How to Pick Partners for Love Addicts

How to Assess for Lovers, Friends, and Family Members
Who Are Available for Love

First Edition 2024

Dedication

This book is dedicated to the little girl who never knew how special she truly was.

May this book help her find the love she always deserved.

May she know how healing, joyful, and full love from the right sources can be

Table of Contents

Shena Lashey, M.MFT

Preface

This guide was written for every warm-hearted person who loved the wrong person a little too much and got burned.

It is for the person who, in a room of a hundred people, somehow still picks the person who will not show up for them the way they need.

I hope that this manual will serve as a guide that you can use to objectively assess all of your relationships to find those which are the healthiest for you until it becomes second nature.

And I hope that this book will teach you the magic art between balancing listening to your heart and your mind.

Shena Lashey, M.MFT

Introduction

Love addicts come ready to love with full hearts. For the people in their inner circles and beyond, the love addict has an abundance of care, empathy, and generosity for those they bond with. They are the ones you want to always have in your corner – forever loyal, generous and forgiving.

Unfortunately for them, the receivers of this love rarely have the same level of fidelity and investment. Somehow, the love addict will repeatedly pick the exact people over and over again who will take this type of love for granted and often exploit it.

This guide aims to break the pattern of both attracting and being attracted to unavailable people by identifying what are healthy signs of availability in a person. Readers will learn to distinguish the difference between signs of unavailability which are dangerous red flags versus minor annoyances that don't render a relationship unsalvageable.

This book is for **all** relationships

Though the examples within will focus primarily on romantic partnerships, and 40 signs of availability and unavailability are the same standards for all their relationships. Whether platonic, familial, romantic, professional, or anything in between, every person needs to be looking for these signs of availability and unavailability in all their primary relationships.

Availability vs Unavailability in a Relationship

When someone has the qualities of availability, the following will happen:

- Your connection and relationship will flourish.
- Your self-esteem and sense of internal safety will grow.
- Your nervous system and previous trauma heal due to being able to co-regulate with healthy and available others (in other words, you no longer have to live on guard in all your relationships).

When someone has the qualities of unavailability, the following will happen:

- Your connection and relationship will have extreme highs and lows, and sometimes, you will feel it come to a standstill.
- Your self-esteem will falter and your sense of internal safety will feel unstable.
- Your need to be hypervigilant for threats to the relationship and yourself will increase

You may find that what you thought were just simple differences in personality and perspective are actually warning signs for future fights and betrayal. Unfortunately, in many cases, they also be warning signs for later abuse.

It is important for love addicts to prioritize learning if a potential friend, partner, or lover is available versus whether they have heavy chemistry. Many love addicts become overly attached to someone with whom they felt intense feelings only to find that this person was destructive to their self esteem and cause deep trauma. Once you determine if a person is available, factors like chemistry and compatibility are appropriate to factor in.

You will have access to The Availability Scale for Relationships © where you will be able to rate where each of your relationships fall in the scale of availability.

This book will also challenge you to **be** the type of person you want to meet by being available yourself. To have relationships that flourish, you must be open and available yourself to let others love you fully.

The fact that you are the defining factor for the types of relationships is great news! It means you have and have always had the power to determine the relationships you want. Even when it has felt impossible and that others had the power, it is only because you stopped focusing on yourself and what you wanted to make way for others. With this book, you'll be able to spot these patterns and break this cycle.

In addition to offering a clear list of all 40 available and unavailable relationship characteristics, this guide will give a full breakdown of each one with examples to connect to your everyday life.

My Wish for You

Dear Reader, you deserve to have healthy and available relationships.

So, let's start off by breaking down what gets in the way and what makes it hard to pick partners as love addicts.

Part 1:
How We Got Here

Shena Lashey, M.MFT

Chapter 1:
What Makes it Hard for Love Addicts to Pick People?

For those of us with so much love to give, what makes it hard to find the people who are ready to receive what we have to share?

To answer this, let's start by breaking down what is love addiction and how it affects us.

Love Addiction is the persistent obsession of a person, relationship, or the fantasy of who you would like that person and relationship to be, and mistaking that intensity (and chemistry) for love.

Love addicts build an over-connection to the fantasy of who a particular person or relationship can be due to their unmet need to feel loved and seen. They believe that the *right* relationship can fix this unmet need and resolve any deeply felt areas of neglect by being in their dream relationship.

As a result, love addicts consistently overgive in all their relationships to overcompensate for and attempt to correct red flags to get such a relationship. Codependency and similar behaviors will exist across all their relational domains (romantic, platonic, and familial) as the need to be connected and loved is immense.

Because of this overwhelming need, they will abandon themselves by compromising on their standards and neglecting any warning signs of danger. Their belief is that their own patience, dedication, and willingness to "own their part" to this relationship will ultimately resolve any relationship issues.

They firmly believe that the relationship person they are addicted to are just a few *minor* tweaks from being perfect. Once everyone is able to move through their own hurdles, true love will win. Their relationship will thrive, and they will finally be able to relax into feeling safe and loved.

However, in a room of a hundred people, the love addict somehow either fixates on or accepts the advances of the one person who will be neglectful and unavailable to their needs. This neglect often mirrors similar patterns of neglect from early childhood trauma or past relationships. They are confused because often the initial chemistry is intense.

Unfortunately, because it is someone who is unavailable, this person will inevitably end up failing them, whether physically, emotionally, mentally, spiritually, financially, or sexually, in the relationship.

As a result, post relationship, this person will leave the love addict feeling confused, used, unwanted, unloved, and completely drained by continuing to give to a relationship without receiving the same in return.

Sometimes, the unavailable person can be described as a "love avoidant." Where the love addict will self-abandon and over-give to attend to the needs of their partner and relationship, the love avoidant will persistently put up walls in intimate relationships to avoid being emotionally overwhelmed and intruded upon. They have a deep need to protect their sense of control and independence. Despite wanting close relationships, they may also see vulnerability as dangerous and intimacy as an overwhelming burden and responsibility. They do their best to block, slow down, and inhibit the relationship from taking over their lives and hearts.

They will try to diffuse the connection with avoidant behaviors, such as:

- Lack of emotional expression
- Over-scheduling and busyness (to reduce time together)
- Pursuing outside relationships (sometimes in the form of cheating in romantic partnerships)
- Picking fights and being highly critical
- Omitting details and hiding parts of their lives

Ironically, they often bond with love addicts who will come in ready to carry the emotional load and labor by craving connection. At first, this is great, but they will often over time come to resent it—desiring that need for freedom and relief. At this point, they will enact their distancing techniques to slow down or temper the progression of the relationship and their responsibility to it. This is distressing to the love addict who wants to get the relationship "back to how it used to be."

Thus, the love addict, instead of severing the relationship, will continue to try to overcome their relationship hurdles by:

- Trying to fix the other person and remedy their red flags
- Understanding the avoidant wants space and becoming *needless* and *wantless* to lessen their burden of taking up space
- Attempting to adopt what the avoidant wants for the relationship standard
- Offering empty threats and ultimatums to leave if there is no change
- Acting as if the blocks in intimacy do not bother them

Despite their best efforts, the love avoidant is not moved by these actions and will remain unavailable to the love addict. For the love avoidant, the love addict was never the problem that they were avoiding, but they were avoiding their own fear of intimacy and connection. These blocks were in place long before their relationship with the love addict started. And they will continue for long afterwards until the love avoidant is ready to deal with the trauma that has made closeness feel unsafe for them. There is nothing the love addict can do to guide or coax them to the other side of their avoidance. In fact, the more they try, the more pressured and resentful the love avoidant may feel.

Thus, it is important to determine which persons come ready and willing to be in a full relationship with us. It is not a love addict's job to fix the person they are with. They deserve to pick relationships that are safe to be fully seen and known with those are that open and ready to do the same.

Love addicts must be on guard from attempting to change themselves to fit another's attachment pattern. The love addict must understand that their desire to be seen, loved, and protected is natural. They are deserving of having those needs met.

It is not that they need to repress these needs, but they must find relationships that are ready and willing to give these actions to them.

Self-Assessment Questions:

- Which qualities of love addiction do you relate to the most?
- Have you found yourself susceptible to mistaking intense feelings for love?
- Are there partners or prior relationships that you have had difficulty removing due to your over attachment?
- Are there some relationships that you have found yourself showing up as more love avoidant?

Chapter 2:
Why Love Addicts Miss Red Flags

As a Therapist and Love Addiction Coach, I have gotten the opportunity to I work with the most amazing, talented, beautiful, loving, spiritual, wise, and caring women in the world.

Their discernment in everyday life is incredible.

They are usually able to identify correctly great career opportunities and situations that will help them prosper. They can even clearly see when there are red flags in potential relationships for friends and loved ones.

However, when it comes to themselves, it's a bit harder.

This is because, as young children, they were often not taught the importance of identifying and validating their own needs. They may have been emotionally neglected, abused, or breadcrumbs of affection by earlier caregivers and loved ones. Thus, over time, they learned how to go without their basic needs of care, protection, and consistency to be provided for.

However, though these needs were not attended to, they never went away. And without knowing what it feels like to have these needs met from a safe source, it makes them overlook early warning signs of neglect or danger in others.

Sometimes this oversight is because they see potential in the other person or believe this relationship to be everything they imagined. They believe that the character flaws are small issues that can be outgrown, managed, avoided, or waited out.

Often, love addicts think that if they keep an eye on these flaws, they can either control the outcome or reduce the consequences should they arise. However, this is never the case. The consequences eventually come, followed by heartbreak and disappointment.

And as lovers of love, sometimes love addicts don't see the flaws at all. All they see is the rose-tinted fantasy they believe the relationship can be.

This blindness to these red flags proves dangerous to the love addict, as this ultimately results in sadness, heartbreak, disappointment, and unexpected trauma that they must now overcome.

Self-Assessment Questions:

- Are you better at seeing the red flags in other relationships better than your own?
- What red flags have you overlooked in the past?
- What do you normally do when you see red flags (see list below)? If any of the items, how has that worked out for you?
    - o try to fix them
    - o ignore them or try to wait them out
    - o try to overcorrect the environment for them

- try to decrease your needs so they don't bother you
- threaten the person to change or you're leaving
- other…

Chapter 3:
Ignored Red Flags, Trauma, and Danger

How do you know if something is a flaw that is relationship-destroying versus a normal human idiosyncrasy that may be simply annoying but not dangerous?

This guide defines flaws as anything that can cause emotional, mental, physical, sexual, spiritual, or financial harm to the person on the receiving end.

For example, a partner who always loves to take the scenic route on a drive where you prefer the quickest path is an example of an imperfection, but not a dangerous flaw. It may add time to your commute and may deeply frustrate you, but it is not going to cause longstanding injury to your emotional, mental, or physical health and esteem.

On the other hand, a partner who is consistently untruthful to you and withholds details may:

- Place you in compromising positions (physical harm)
- Make you doubt your sense of sanity due to gaslighting (mental harm)
- Hurt your sense of self-worth (emotional harm) by undervaluing your feelings

When They Don't Know What They Are Doing

Sometimes someone's flaws are not fully apparent to them.

Despite their impact on others, these behaviors may be traits that were normalized and passed down by previous caretakers. They may also be patterns they picked up for survival due to their own history of trauma and heartbreak.

However, the reason for these harmful traits may give you information about their history, but it *does not* excuse them.

A love addict's only job is to determine if the actions of the other person are harmful to them. This does not mean you are judging them or saying they are a bad person. They are rightfully prioritizing their own needs and safety, which are valuable and deserving of being attended to. Once you have that information, the love addict can then decide how they would like to proceed in the relationship.

Your Imperfections Do Not Mean You Deserve Less

"Nobody is perfect" is usually the reframe I hear from love addicts attempting to excuse the bad behaviors of those in their lives. This phrase is often followed by "And I'm not perfect either."

Even upon seeing the red flags and impact of the bad behaviors from others, they question how they can rightfully, have higher standards for their relationships when they are so clearly imperfect themselves.

Thus, out of *fairness* and *self-accountability*, they feel compelled to be patient with this person's flaws. Because, in the same way, they would want this person to forgive them for being *a complete mess*.

This low view of themselves is what makes love addicts more susceptible to accepting crumbs of *good* behaviors because someone like *them* couldn't hope to expect more. Higher expectations don't match what they feel they are worthy of receiving.

Unfortunately, love addicts give this open-ended forgiveness and understanding to those who least deserve it—the unavailable. Those who are unavailable are not able to fully appreciate and receive this sacrifice.

However, the love addict hopes that by forgiving them, seeing the best in them, communicating their needs patiently, and giving them another chance, the unavailable person will be grateful. Even better, the love addict hopes that the unavailable person will be inspired to change and feel appreciative of the pure love being bestowed upon them.

But this is not the case. The unavailable person either does not have the needs of the love addict on their radar or does not have the capacity to fulfill them. A love addict's self-abandonment does not inspire any change on their part.

In fact, I have often heard those who have been on the receiving end of one's self-abandonment actually wish that this person would stand up for themselves and have more self-respect for their needs.

The love addict's lack of confidence is not endearing to someone who is unavailable. Sometimes, it makes them feel pity, and even have less respect for the love addict.

Your "Love" Cannot Heal Their Flaws... and It's Also Not Your Job to Try

In spite of signs the unavailable person is not in the right place to change, the love addict is very fixated on this person and the relationship working out. Thus, they will do what they can to try to make it work which may include trying to heal the unavailable person with their unconditional love and forgiveness.

Unfortunately, you cannot *love* someone out of their own defensiveness, avoidance, and trauma response, should they not be ready to look at it. That is work they must do for themselves by their own initiation.

Not holding others to standards of respect, love, and consistency does not help them grow. It actually teaches them that it is okay for them to treat you in this way, AND they can get everything they want be acting the way that they are.

Making yourself a doormat and revolving door of endless forgiveness actually *reinforces* the bad behavior. It doesn't cure it.

Should the loving approach fail, you cannot threaten or coerce anyone into doing anything. Any initial compliance, because it is not based on their own desire to change, will either:

- not be maintained long-term as it's not self-generated or they will come to resent you for pushing change on them that they did not want

What Should Love Addicts Do With Forgiveness and Grace

The love addict's best use for that compassion and acceptance is to turn it towards themselves. Know that *they are* worthy of relationships that leave them better than they found them.

It is best for love addicts to remember that there is only one set of decisions they can control: their own. They have complete ownership over who they allow themselves to be intimate with and determine who does not make the cut.

When Everyone Before You Has Hurt You

If love addicts find themselves consistently in relationships with people who harm them, some of the information that follows in this guide may be surprising. There may be a list of qualities that you thought were mildly annoying. But, serious red flags? Never.

However, if a love addict has a history of abuse or emotional neglect, this lack of awareness is due to these types of flaws being normalized, growing up. So, as an adult, what are clearly seen as dangerous and harmful by others, are just personality quirks, par for the course, and part of the *normal* ups and downs of relationships, to a love addict.

In this guide, we will learn to reset our standards so that all connections are built from a healthy and true foundation so that the relationship can flourish.

Self-Assessment Questions

- What are some common needs you have overlooked in the past to keep a relationship?
- What are common red flags you have noticed in previous relationships?
- In the past, how have you tried to fix partners or relationships that were not showing up for you like you needed?
- Have you ever had a partner, friend, or family member who told you that you deserved more than what you were accepting from them? If so, how did you receive it when they told this to you (i.e. as a compliment, as a push to be more confident, as an insult, etc.)?

Part 2:
Breaking Down Availability vs. Unavailability

Shena Lashey, M.MFT

Chapter 4:
Pre-Assessing Your Primary Relationships

Before we get into the signs of availability versus unavailability, let's pre-assess your current relationships for their availability.

Instructions:
List your top three primary relationships and their connection to you. They can be past or current romantic partners, family members, friends, professional relationships, or any combination of the above.

i.e., Mom–my mother, Mike–My partner, Teresa–My best friend, Sam–My ex situationship who I try to be "friends" with

Name   **Relationship to You**

_____   _____

_____   _____

_____   _____

Rate Your Relationships

On a scale of 0 to 5, where would you rank your primary loved ones as far as how well they attend to your needs (i.e. emotional, mental, spiritual, sexual, physical, financial, etc.).

Then answer the questions below, assessing why you gave this ranking, the ways this relationship benefits or challenges you, and whether you should want to keep this relationship as it is or change it.

You may use another sheet of paper to write your answers if needed.

Relationship #1: _____

1	2	3	4	5
Unavailable				Available

Why did I give them this ranking?

What are the ways this relationship benefits me?

What are the ways this relationship may harm me?

Are there any compromises I have made for this relationship that I regret or wish were different?

Would I like to move closer to this person, keep it the same, or create distance?

Relationship #2: _____

1	2	3	4	5
Unavailable				Available

Why did I give them this ranking?

What are the ways this relationship benefits me?

What are the ways this relationship may harm me?

Are there any compromises I have made for this relationship that I regret or wish were different?

Would I like to move closer to this person, keep it the same, or create distance?

Relationship #3: _____

1	?	3	4	5
Unavailable				Available

Why did I give them this ranking?

What are the ways this relationship benefits me?

What are the ways this relationship may harm me?

Are there any compromises I have made for this relationship that I regret or wish were different?

Would I like to move closer to this person, keep it the same, or create distance?

Being clear about how you see each of your relationships, what is working and what is not, is the first step in gaining clarity on whether it is meeting your emotional, mental, and relational needs.

Now that you have a starting assessment, let's look at the actual signs of availability and unavailability to fully evaluate your relationships.

Chapter 5:
Availability – What You're Looking For

Availability is the state of being open to emotional connection, intimacy, vulnerability, and one's physical presence. The available person is attentive to who you are, sees you fully, and finds value in helping you find joy in your life. They enjoy themselves when you are around and express that to you. They are self-knowledgeable and expressive with their own thoughts and needs.

Because they take care of themselves, they can find space for you as well. With an available person, the relationship is natural and easy.

Close relationships with available people are a healing balm to our souls. Your heart and your emotional mind deserve to be protected and to be in relationships that provide ease. Your emotional state matters. You, as a person, matters. And the love you have available to give matters too.

When you give your heart, devotion, and time to those who will waste and abuse it, not only is it unloving to yourself; it also makes it difficult to share your love freely and openly with others. It makes it difficult to trust.

If you consistently pick unavailable people to befriend, build a romantic relationship with, and prioritize connection within your family, you will start to believe that all humans are hopelessly untrustworthy, tainted, and unavailable. Even worse, you will start to believe that you are unworthy, hopelessly flawed, and undeserving of true, rich, faithful, and healthy love.

In truth, healthy and available people who are fun, self-accountable, honest, and want the best for you exist! You, as you are, are worthy of those relationships! However, you just must find them and be available to them, yourself, for connection.

The first step to finding available people is to learn how to identify and disconnect from those who are unavailable and drain your energy.

You must stop spending time on those who cannot, don't know how to, or just plain don't want to show up for you in the way you need.

This also clears the way for you to be available for the type of love and connection you want as well.

Some may prefer to *stick it out* with someone who is unavailable because of the time and history invested in them. To move on would be to *abandon* all their hard work, and they fear the moment they leave is when the person finally gets it together. They are sick at the thought of missing this opportunity to get everything they want.

However, the "sunken time" fallacy is just that—a fallacy. It is not a waste of time for you to walk away from someone who is not the right fit.

You are actually reclaiming your self-esteem, mental stability, and your TIME by making space to be in the relationships that build you up.

By correctly categorizing your relationships, you are also reclaiming your power by walking towards what works for you versus what destroys you.

Chapter 6:
The 40 Signs of Availability and Unavailability

Here are the 20 signs of availability and 20 signs of unavailability to make 40 signs in total.

They will be defined in more detail in the following chapters, but for now, here is the list of each type of signs.

Available Qualities	Unavailable Qualities
Respects your boundaries	Intrusive and does not respect your boundaries
Truthful	Deceptive and/or tells half-truths
Non-judgmental	Highly critical and insulting
Protective/defends you from others	Talks about you behind your back/does not protect you

Fun to be around (according to what is fun for you)	Emotionally draining to be around
Treats you the same no matter who is around	Inconsistent in their kindness toward you (nice to you in some places but mean to you in others)
Giving and generosity is not quid pro quo	Only wants to receive from you, never gives/counts what has been given vs. received
Keeps their commitments to you	Flaky and does not follow through with commitments
Makes time for you and their other commitments	May ghost you when they find something better
Happy for you when you shine	Competitive and jealous, one-ups you
Supportive of your endeavors	Unsupportive of your endeavors
May ask for support but does their personal work on their own feelings as well	Uses you to emotionally dump their issues
Emotionally open	Emotionally cut off and reserved
Holds space for your feelings when you're upset	Withholds love and affection, and cuts you off when you set an appropriate boundary
Does not personalize when you disagree with them	Turns your feelings of hurt from their behaviors back onto you

Initiates and listens to what is going on with you	Crowds you out and only focuses on themselves
Appreciative	Entitled and expects you to give
Able to compromise	Controlling
Includes you in events and important moments	Excludes and leaves you out
Genuinely likes and enjoys you as a person	Disinterested in you and/or seems to just tolerate you

The Availability versus Unavailability list is not a "Pros and Cons" list. Each availability characteristic is not equal in weight to an unavailability characteristic.

The items on the availability list are integral components to a safe and healthy relationship. Without them present, you will feel depleted emotionally, mentally, socially, spiritually, and financially.

The unavailability list includes qualities that are emotionally, mentally, and spiritually dangerous, harmful, and abusive. They do not hold the same weight as innocuous quirks, such as chewing with their mouth open or telling off-beat jokes. Yes, those types of qualities may be mildly annoying based on your tolerance level, but those kinds of habits will not make or break a relationship.

All qualities within the unavailability list, if they exist in a relationship, contribute to the deterioration of a partnership. And they also affect the self-esteem and self-worth of the person on the receiving end— you!

As such, they should not solely be seen as cons, but more aptly as big bright red warning signs of danger.

In other words, if each availability characteristic is worth +10 point, the unavailability characteristics should be worth -50 each due to their longstanding impact. Again, they do not offset each other.

You will learn about how to rank your relationships according to their availability with "The Availability Scale for Relationships" later in this guide.

Signs of Availability vs. Compatibility

Signs of availability also do not equal compatibility. You can meet someone who is super healthy and available for you, but your sense of humor completely clashes. You may have different interests in hobbies or have different life goals. If you tried to force a friendship or relationship with them, you would actually still be operating from an unhealthy unavailable stance. Because you're trying to make a relationship happen with someone who is not the right fit for you or your lifestyle.

Similarly, you can meet someone who completely cracks you up, loves the exact hobbies you have, shares the same fashion interests, and expresses the same goals. But if they are dishonest, flaky, vindictive, manipulative, and run hot and cold, this relationship will cause emotional trauma and damage to your self-esteem and ability to trust. This is also an unavailable relationship where the initial pleasure will not be offset by the harm.

Compatibility between personality differences, temperaments, cultural norms, spiritual beliefs, sense of humor, love languages, etc., will vary between people. Meaning you will have to find those who click the best with you and who are *also* available for connection. If the relationship is not foundationally safe and uplifting, it will not flourish and thrive.

If you meet someone with whom you have incredible chemistry but is unavailable, the temptation to ignore the red flags will be strong. As a love addict, you must remember that this world is abundant, and it is absolutely possible for you to find relationships that have both of these qualities. You do not have to sacrifice yourself and your sanity any longer for temporary moments of pleasure that are followed by pain.

You get to have it all and it gets to be easy.

So, let's learn how to evaluate the qualities we want in partners. Let's learn about the Signs of Availability.

Self-Assessment Questions

- Have you ever confused intense chemistry with someone as a sign that they were also healthy and available for you?
- Have you ever had intense chemistry with someone who was healthy and as well? How was that relationship different from others?
- Have you ever tried to make a relationship work with someone who was a "nice person" but that you had little in common with? How did that relationship work out?

Shena Lashey, M.MFT

Chapter 7:
Signs of Availability

The following are signs of availability for you to assess in your relationships.

All of these are indicators that this person may be emotionally, physically, spiritually, financially, and sexually nurturing for you as a friend, partner, colleague, etc.

You may use the *How to Pick Partners for Love Addicts Workbook* companion guide to actively rank and score your current and former relationships.

Respects your boundaries

This person knows what feels safe for you and your limits, and honors them. They do not force or guilt you to change them to accommodate their own comfort level or what they want. They are intentionally considerate and may actively anticipate how to show up within the guidelines of what makes you feel safe and supported.

They also maturely express their boundaries and needs to you. If you breach their boundaries, they can have a respectful conversation with you about what happened and what they prefer to happen instead.

If what you are asking for contradicts their own personal boundaries and needs, they can communicate this to you respectfully, without blame and accusation, as well. You have cooperative conversations to find compromise when it aligns with what you both want. If you're not able to make a compromise, you are able to determine if the relationship needs to be adjusted or may not be the best fit.

Kindness and curiosity are at the forefront of all boundary conversations.

Truthful

This person tells you the full truth about their emotions, motives, and thoughts when asked. You can trust that they are giving full context and not omitting important information.

You are fully confident that the story you are receiving does not have extraneous details that would change your experience of what you are being told.

Honesty is a core value they hold in their relationship with you and is not something that must be pressured or forced out.

Bear in mind that truthfulness is not a pass for the person being unkind. While we may have truth-tellers in our lives who may vary in the strength of their blunt honesty and forthrightness, it is never a pass to be verbally abusive.

Sometimes, someone will give you tough and direct feedback. It may sting a bit, but you can still feel supported, seen, and believed in, on the other side of it. You are inspired to make decisions for yourself because you have been reminded of your value and what you deserve. You feel empowered and seen.

However, sometimes feedback that is brutally honest may motivate change—but at an emotional cost. You may end up feeling more condemned than encouraged. It may leave you may feeling criticized, disempowered, ashamed, and judged.

Non-judgmental

With these people, you feel free to be yourself—quirks, a sense of humor, challenging thoughts—all of it! They can hold space for you and accept you for who you are.

Their acceptance extends to hard moments, or if there is a characteristic discovered where you need to grow. Because they love you, they may give you honest critical feedback, but it will be in support of you as opposed to condemnation. They can separate your actions from who you are, and you are able to feel they are doing so by how they treat you and talk to you.

Even if they believe you could have handled a situation differently, they are still able to retain empathy and care for you, despite their disagreement.

They typically refrain from making assumptions about you. However, if they have an inference, they will check in with you to see if it is true without jumping to conclusions about your thoughts, emotions, and intentions.

Protective/defends you from others

This person does what they can to protect your value, dignity, mental health, emotional health, and physical body in their interactions with you.

They ensure they speak positively about you and protect your image and reputation. They defend you from those who may make disparaging remarks and do not make fun of you to foster a bond with other people.

They may, depending on the situation and context, protect you from being harmed by either removing you from potentially dangerous situations or physically getting in the way of a threat. This person sees you as a treasure.

In intimate moments, they are cognizant of your feelings and your thoughts. Even if things get heated during a disagreement, they can communicate their anger and disappointment without hitting below the belt. They understand the severity of words and actively ensure they are protective of your heart without you having to force them to do so.

Emotionally available and open

This person shares their emotions and thoughts about what is happening in their life. The focus is not the number of words and frequency with which they do this. Some people are naturally more talkative than others. Instead, they are open and available for expressing themselves.

They actively share their thoughts, especially if it pertains to your relationship, and do not expect you to mind-read. If they have a concern, they are open to broaching the topic with you or discussing it with you if you introduce it.

They may be a person of few words, but in their brevity, they are honest and vulnerable with their thoughts. You do not have to guess where you stand with them, and they invite you into their emotional world because they feel safe. This invitation into their world may involve them initiating and sharing their hopes, fears, dreams, and emotional needs with you.

While all the Availability Qualities in this guide are best expressed in relationships where the other person (you) is exhibiting this quality as well, this is perhaps where it is most important this balance exists.

If you:

1) are unable to hold space for this person's emotions
2) often discount their emotions and call them immature, silly, or fake
3) judge their emotions and experiences as not being as important as your own
4) use your own biases on how certain genders are *allowed* to feel about certain topics and heartbreaks
5) are prone to telling someone how they feel, without listening

This will shut the most open person down.

Be sure to work on your own ability to hold the tough emotions of others. Work through your own biases where necessary, to be a safe place for this person as well.

Treats you the same, no matter who's around

This person is just as kind, loving, supportive, doting, and attentive when you are alone as when you are in public. They are as protective as they are when their friends, family members, and colleagues are around.

This person likes you openly, both in private and in public. They are consistent in their treatment of you, and it is not something you ever have to correct or be hypervigilant of.

If you are a couple who banters and playfully pokes fun at each other, it is mutual and done with mutually understood limits in mind. The tone is equal, and they do not belittle you to elevate their social status.

Even in their jokes, you feel the warmth and the sense of being known. As it is mutual, you can receive it as well, and it does not escalate for show, should others be present.

Supportive of your endeavors

This person is excited to see you go out for the things that are important to you. Whether it is a hobby, a vocation change, exploring a talent, using your voice and showing up for yourself, or anything in between, they are happy for you as you go after your dreams.

Support can look like verbal affirmation and celebration, such as:

- "Good job! I always knew you could do it."
- "That sounds amazing. Go for it!"

A supportive person in your circle will do the following to support you:

- Emotionally, by motivating you via care and consideration
- Security-wise, by providing a safe space to land if you're feeling discouraged after failing or hitting a setback
- Validation-wise, by believing in your dreams and verbally letting you know that you can do it
- Physically, by showing up for you and attending important moments and events
- Financially, by sponsoring your endeavors or encouraging you to stay persistent by connecting you to relevant resources

All types of support are not necessary at the same time. However, no matter the method, you can tell they are in your corner.

As a self-aware person, themselves, they know that having your own wants, needs, and interests is necessary for both your health and the health of the relationship. They love and appreciate how your interests make you more dynamic and see your individuality and success as a source of admiration and not as a threat.

Keeps their commitments to you

With this person, you can trust that when they say they are going to show up, to provide a favor, or do a task for you, they will do so. It is important for them to show up and be a consistent source of support in your life.

You can trust their word and that they will not flake on their commitment to you when something better comes along or just because they have changed their mind.

You understand that in life, things happen, and every person has full ownership to change their mind, say no, re-evaluate their capacity, and pivot. However, in regard to this qualifier, their need to pivot is the exception rather than the norm.

You know the availability of this person, and they do their best to provide you with the security and safety of consistency.

See the "Special Considerations" chapter for notes on the impact of neurodivergent disorders on this quality.

Giving and generosity is not quid pro quo

They give gifts, offer care, share compliments, and make compromises because your happiness brings them joy—not because they expect anything in return, now or later.

They do not tally marks of favors or consistently talk about what is fair and unfair when asked for something.

This person is open to meeting your needs and making you feel safe, seen, and appreciated. They feel you deserve this treatment because of the value you add to their life for being who you are. You do not have to earn their kindness.

In relationships that are open and generous, you feel free to ask for what you need and want, without fear of retaliation later.

Makes time for you and their other commitments

This person prioritizes spending time with you. Even when they are really busy, they may find a way to stay in contact with you. Some examples may look like:

- Texts/phone calls in between meetings
- Regular check-ins, sharing their day, and asking about yours
- Initiates making firm plans to connect at a later date

This prioritization is seen as a gift and not a burden. They are excited to see you instead of just communicating verbally. Nor do they hint that they feel obligated to spend this time with you.

Friendly or romantic dates that are scheduled actually happen or are intentionally rescheduled if mishaps or time conflicts occur. Based on individual preferences, these dates can be virtual, telephonic, or in-person. The important component is that this is quality time for the two of you to connect.

Sometimes, you may meet a person who does not have the capacity to see you often, but will still try to make you a priority with the limited time and energy they have. For example, they may have a job that legitimately requires 80 hours per week or they may be a single parent of multiple children. Thus, they may make intentional plans to connect, but the moments have much space in between.

You must decide if what you receive is enough to keep this person in your life, and modify your expectations according to their capacity. Are these true deal-breakers?

A busy person may not be unhealthy and unavailable to you, but their lack of time may not align with what you want.

If you decide to keep this relationship, it is important to ensure you are taking care of your own emotional and social needs in other places and relationships. Charging one person to be your only emotional source of support can be a heavy burden, even when both persons are time-available.

Is happy when you shine

This person is ecstatic and over the moon when good things are happening for you. They are your biggest cheerleaders. They find joy when good things happen to you and want to see you receive more and more blessings and abundance.

They feel and communicate these beliefs to you and think that there is no one more deserving. They offer best-case scenarios when good things are happening for you rather than the things that can go wrong.

They do not "yes-but" your accomplishments, nor do they feel the need to be competitive and one-up you when good things are happening for you. They do not feel threatened by the good happening to you, as they know your path is your own, and they can hold joy and cheer for your abundance.

Holds space for your feelings when you're upset

The available person knows that your feelings are valuable. They will allow you to feel your emotions without punishing you for them, treating you or your feelings like a burden, and allowing you to explore what you feel.

This may look like a listening ear without judgment.

A person who holds space does not necessarily need to agree with your sentiments and mirror them exactly. However, as an available person, they understand that your experience is your own. That you have the right to feel how you need to feel. They do not attribute mean or dehumanizing labels to you, even if you disagree.

If you are experiencing negative feelings and the available person is a part of the reason, they can hold space for you. If they have a different experience, they can share so without insults and emotional abuse.

If the conflict is solvable, you can find a resolution through conversation, where you are both seeking to understand the other person's point of view. You can also share what you need and feel individually, as well.

Does not personalize when you disagree

This person welcomes hearing your thoughts, emotions, and beliefs even when they may conflict with their own. They are happy that you have your own mind and personality, and find pleasure in you, being you.

They respect that you own your identity while also having a healthy connection to their own identity and needs. You can have your own opinions and still stay in the relationship.

In moments when your needs or desires clash with their own, they do not take it as a personal attack. They will not attempt to shame, guilt, or coerce you to change your boundaries, beliefs, and opinions.

As a healthy person, they will own their personal needs, boundaries, and beliefs, and communicate as needed, with honesty. If the situation requires it, you can discuss your competing interests with mutual respect.

May ask for support but does their own personal work to own their feelings as well

This person may see you as an emotional resource and ask you for feedback and advice. They may see you as a trusted confidant, but you are also not their be-all and end-all for emotional support.

Their ability to cope does not rely solely on you being available to listen to their trauma stories. This frees you from feeling overwhelmed with responsibility to them.

This person has a healthy balance of vulnerability, openness, and camaraderie with you. They can openly share what is going on with them and places where they are in need, but can also be self-accountable and find solutions on their own. And, when they do find solutions, they do their best to follow through and implement them to make their lives better instead of living in excuses.

Initiates and listens to what is going on with you

This person cares what is going on in your world. They will ask how your day was and listen. They will ask follow-up questions. They will remember to ask you about it later.

When you are going through a hard time, they will empathize with you and attempt to support you. If they know that you are the type who prefers space rather than a lot of attention when going through trials, they will intentionally support you in the way you prefer.

When asking how things are going with you, they are not listening absentmindedly, waiting for their turn to jump in. They can stay present with your story, validate your emotions, and ask follow-up questions.

Your conversations are easy and non-competitive, with space for both to share as much or as little as you want, and you are mutually interested in each other's well-being.

Able to compromise

This person is open to not only hearing what you want and need but also open to compromise, to meet you where you are.

This is different from appeasing. Appeasing is common for those who are not fully connected to their own confidence, wants, and values. Because of this, they are more willing to go along with what you want, to placate you. Though seemingly mutual at the time, this is a recipe for future resentment for the one who is placating.

Someone who balances self-confidence with understanding can truly hear your needs and work toward compromise. Because they care, they are willing to compromise, which means either:

- adopt what you want and finding a middle ground where both sides can be happy
- or continue to stand in their own preference while validating why your needs and preferences are just as important

In a relationship with this person, it is not always *their way*, just like it's not always *your way*. However, they see you getting your needs met as a happy benefit to them because they care about your emotional well-being.

Their attitude toward compromise is generous, and they can balance aligning their own boundaries by meeting you where you are.

Includes you in important events and milestones

This person either physically includes you in the important spaces of their life or expresses openly what is happening with them. They do not hide information or keep you from their life.

They take the initiative to see you and include you in important moments. They introduce you to people who matter to them, and show pride in having you in their life.

When you are at these events, in front of others, you are treated as an asset, a joy, not a liability and a burden. They are excited that you are there with them, rather than being resentful or annoyed.

And even though they want you around, it is healthy for them to have their own interests, hobbies, and friendships—outside of their connection with you. You are not required to be in attendance for every event, hobby, and moment in their life.

However, the point of this quality is that you are: 1) not hidden, and 2) they are not hiding information about their life from you. An activity or hobby may be their own—their personal escape that is sacred and only for them. But it will not be a secret.

They may have outside friendships and relationships, but neither you nor the nature of their relationships with others or their level of closeness are secrets.

Appreciative

This person sees the value you bring to their life and that you value them as well. They appreciate your presence and see your relationship as a gift. They find value in what you bring to the relationship primarily through your sense of self (just you, being you!). Any other resources you bring (i.e. reputation, money, network, humor, etc.) are extras on top of you just being who you are. You are enough for them, and they show so through their actions.

We can look at the five love languages for examples of how this appreciation may be expressed. In his book *The 5 Love Languages*, author Gary Chapman asserts that all people give and receive in one of five distinct "love languages."

Chapman states that the five ways that people give and receive love are: Words of Affirmation, Gifts, Acts of Service, Quality Time, and Physical Touch. They are described as the following:

- If their primary love language comes in the form of Words of Affirmation, this person will give you lots of verbal gratitude and words of appreciation. You will always know they see you and are thankful to you.
- If their language is Gifts, it may look like thoughtful little trinkets or larger items to show they are thinking about you.
- Acts of Service may look like doing tasks for you that make

your life easier. They are intentional about trying to help you and are available physically, for support.

- Quality Time looks like seeking moments to be with you, even if you're not doing much at all. Because you are one of *their people*, just being in your presence is enough.
- Physical Touch may look like lots of touches, hugs, and kisses. These touches can be purely affectionate to feel connected to you. They do not have to have a sexual connotation, even in a romantic partnership. These touches are how they show intimacy.

These love languages may be the same as ours or a different one. To maintain a healthy relationship and to help the other person feel loved, it is important that we recognize the language the other person prefers to receive, in addition to speaking in our own primary language.

To spot this appreciation, it is important to pay attention to how this person treats you in their own love language and not purely your own. Though you absolutely have a right to want to be loved and appreciated in a certain way, if you are hyper-focused on what you think it should look like, you may miss out on the fact that this person is actively valuing you. That they are showing you love in the best way they know how.

As an available person yourself, remember to express your appreciation to them for how they love and appreciate you. Healthy relationships are best when reciprocal.

Fun to be around (according to what is fun for you)

This person brings joy into your life. There is laughter and fun. This laughter and fun may be quiet and more subdued, or it may be loud and raunchy. It can be sweet and good-natured, or when you two get together, you may have a dry sense of humor or throw around jokes that are not safe for work.

No matter the flavor, you two get each other, mutually enjoy each other, and feel pleasure in each other's presence. You have genuine fun, and truly enjoy yourself when you are spending time with them.

Codependent people struggle with focusing on their own needs and enjoyment. They will overprioritize the satisfaction and security of others even to their own detriment. Because they don't have a connection to their own internal compass for what is pleasurable and safe for them, they will over-rely on the validation and experiences of others to tell them that they are safe or are doing a good job.

For recovering codependents, be mindful to not equate your enjoyment in taking care of this person to be the same as having fun with them.

Some codependents feel most at home with those they get to mother and nurture. Thus, these relationships can be reflexively described as fun because they feel pleasure in being needed and helping the other person.

However, an available relationship must be mutually beneficial and equal on all levels. Ask yourself:

- Am I amused during and after my interactions with this person?
- Do I ever find myself needing to censor what I want to say?
- Do I ever find myself needing to overlook their jokes and their sense of humor that may be offensive, insulting, or not on-brand with what I find funny?
- Is my heart lighter after I spend time with them or more burdened and conflicted?
- Do I feel more expanded, open, and free when I am around this person?
- Do I feel completely free to be myself around them?

Fun and pleasure are just as important as the other qualities of respect, loyalty, and emotional safety. This quality adds depth to relationships, making them well-rounded and fulfilling rather than just functional.

Genuinely likes and enjoys you as a person

This person lights up when you are in their presence. They seem to authentically enjoy conversations and quality time with you, and they express this to you directly.

You can either tell via their light energy or because they have told you specifically that they find you to be a special person in their life. They may have commented that just by being who you are and living fully in your personality, your interests, your humor and insight, you add to their life and make it better.

They like and appreciate you for who you are, not what you can do for them.

Self-Assessment Questions

- Did you learn any positive signs of availability that you hadn't previously considered? Which ones?
- Which signs of availability do your current relationships excel in?
- Which signs of availability do you currently excel in?
- Which signs of availability would you like to find in future relationships?

Chapter 8: Signs of Unavailability

The following are signs of unavailability for you to assess in your relationships.

All of these are indicators that this person may be emotionally, physically, spiritually, financially, and sexually dangerous for you as a friend, partner, colleague, etc.

You may use the *How to Pick Partners Workbook* companion guide to rank and score your current and former relationships.

Intrusive and does not respect your boundaries

The person is more focused on what they want and need in the moment and what would make them feel more comfortable versus of your needs. Their convenience is prioritized.

This can look like:

- pushing you to do something, make an agreement, go somewhere, provide a favor that you do not want to do
- wanting to force a conversation that you are not ready for

mentally and emotionally in the moment
- continuing to ask you questions that make you feel uncomfortable
- attempting to assert control over your actions and thoughts
- bringing up topics that you have shared makes you uncomfortable repeatedly after being asked to stop
- downplaying your rightful show and display of discomfort

To downplay your right to show discomfort, they may:

- state you are being too sensitive. Example statements may include:
  o "You are taking this too sensitively."
  o "I have a right to share what I need with you/You're so selfish and only care about what you want."
- blame you for misinterpreting their statements. Example rebuttals may include:
  o "I'm only trying to help."
  o "I'm only saying this because I love you."
- state that talking about your needs at all is you being selfish. Examples of blame include:
  o "You only care about yourself."
  o "What about me? What I want matters too."

Sometimes, when someone is intrusive, they are very adept at exploiting therapeutic vocabulary to gaslight you and get you to comply.

For example:

- "I feel like you are not honoring my boundaries. I feel really unheard right now."
- "I feel really sad when you do not listen to me."
- "I'm taking ownership of my part and being self-accountable (while actively being insulting and attacking towards you)."

Weaponizing these positive terms and catchphrases will make you think that *you* are the one who is being too sensitive or unreasonable. It is a tactic to get you to comply with their request after your initial refusals.

The connotation being that if you were truly invested in the relationship and a good person, you would take a look in the mirror and realize you were being selfish. You are being asked to give in to their desires and requests in spite of how it makes you feel, emotionally.

Deceptive and/or tells half-truths

This person may frequently lie and contort details to fit their agenda. You are not sure if you are getting the full story or a partial story. Is it a real story, a complete fabrication, or something in the middle?

When giving partial stories, they may answer with limited details or completely omit relevant facts. They may attempt to blame you for not asking them questions in the right way. So, it becomes your fault that you do not have all the information rather than being due to their lack of transparency.

However, they may simultaneously fault you at times for asking them too many questions, insinuating that you do not trust them. You are caught in a "damned if you do, damned if you don't" loop. You do not have the clarifying information you need to feel safe, but you are restricted in terms of the questions you feel allowed to ask, without rebuke. If you do, you will be accused of being an unsupportive partner, family member, or friend.

Some who have been experiencing deception for some time may try to *catch* this person in the act, to reclaim some sense of dignity. They want to validate that they are not *crazy* and have physical proof to validate their concerns in future arguments.

Though this is an understandable reaction, you must realize these efforts are futile. If the person is narcissistic or a master manipulator, they will masterfully take your "gotchas" and turn them around on you, leaving you somehow feeling at fault or embarrassed.

Being faced with proof is not guaranteed to force them to be truthful and repentant. It is also not a guarantee for them to see, finally, the emotional impact of their deception on your mental health.

Those who are consistently deceptive have honed their ability to remain in control and get what they want, despite the consequences. Just because you are bothered by their tactics, and are in emotional distress does not mean that they are.

You must simply assess if you can trust them. You must resist the urge to try to change them or teach them how to live with integrity. That is not your job.

We will talk in later chapters about what *is* your job and what you can actually control.

Highly critical and insulting

This person is very open about telling you the ways that you are falling short. They give you *feedback* when your outfit doesn't look up to par, your hair is unsatisfactory, you stutter during your presentation, and so on.

The highly critical and insulting person may say that they are sharing these thoughts because they are trying to *help* you. They may paint it as if they are the only ones who *truly* care for you. That only they will tell you the truth, while others may lie or skirt around the issue.

If they relate to being the *truth tellers* of their community, they may proudly state that this is how they are. They don't sugarcoat and *won't* sugarcoat their beliefs. They state that those who choose to be around them must be ready to take it.

Truth and feedback from our loved ones are signs of healthy communication in available relationships. However, there is a difference between honest feedback versus cruelty—the abusive belief system that to build someone up, you must tear them down through humiliation or using them as a verbal punching bag.

Critiques from the unavailable person are the norm. If there is a positive comment, it is a backhanded one followed by a "but" right afterwards to discount it. Compliments are so uncommon that it is overlooked or not trusted. Every conversation is riddled with ways that you are falling short or how you could improve.

Unfortunately, often these highly critical individuals are this way because this behavior was modeled to them in how to interact with others. Perhaps, they were highly criticized as a child, and now, they do not know how to be kind. They may also project their own sense of low self-worth onto others as they feel they can never measure up. Jealousy often takes the form of faux confidence.

However, be mindful to not take this bit of insight as a cue for you to help them heal. You do not need to use your energy to inform them of their possible trauma, nor try to appease them by *killing them with kindness.*

Like all insights given here, this is only shared for you to understand that this behavior started way before you and is bigger than your relationship with them. Their journey to heal and unlearn these patterns must happen on their own time when *they* deem it a problem, not you.

Your only goal here is to determine how you feel when this person treats you in this way. Do you leave your interactions feeling taken care of and safe?

Instead of focusing on how you can better this relationship, your energy is best spent by:

- Changing your mindset to understand that even if this type of behavior has been common in your circles, it is not normal

- Improving your own boundaries to restrict those who are verbally and emotionally abusive from having easy access to you
- Finding relationships with people who are automatically open and kind towards you

Talks about you behind your back/does not protect you

This person may swear undying loyalty to you and talk often about how they will protect you and how much you deserve to be loved. But when faced with an opportunity to stand up for you, they do not step up to the plate.

This can look like being a participant in group chats, where you are being discussed in a hurtful way, and they are a bystander. They are not attempting to shut it down, talk about its inappropriateness, or defend you.

To you, they may say, "I didn't know what to say," and apologize for dropping the ball. They may also speak about not wanting to get in the middle of fights between others as part of their own personal values. However, they will badmouth those who slandered you, to show that they are on *your side*.

In real-life scenarios, they may also go silent when loved ones or others are making fun of you, using you as the butt of a joke, or highlighting insecurity. If pressured by you, they may make a half-hearted attempt at telling people to stop. However, their body language and tone may make it obvious that this is not something they truly want to do.

They may also bully you, using you as the butt of the joke, or kidding about how annoying and problematic you are. How they have to deal with a lot by being in a relationship with you. When confronted with how hurtful and humiliating this is, they may tell you that you are being too sensitive and that they are only joking. They may also dismiss your feelings saying, "No one else was thinking like that," or this is just how they are—a straight shooter or that they have a dry sense of humor.

It is easy to excuse someone's failure to stand up for you—maybe they're shy or introverted. Maybe they are have a tough time with family or friends. But when you are evaluating if someone is truly available and ready to support you, these reasons should not cloud your judgment.

Here is the truth: though it may be challenging for them to defend you, a relationship with someone who will protect your well-being, physically, mentally, and emotionally is something you deserve. Someone who is not available, willing or ready to offer you this support, is not someone you want or need.

Another red flag to watch out for are signs that they regularly speak poorly about you to family members or former partners. This behavior goes beyond the occasional vent or seeking advice about conflicts. This is an ongoing pattern of criticism. You might notice them bonding with others over shared complaints about you.

Your well-being matters and you deserve protection in all domains of your life. If your partner repeatedly compromises your privacy and reputation to bond with others or to justify themselves, be alert and pay attention.

Emotionally cut off and reserved

This person is not very open with their emotions. They may not know how to express what they need or do not want to share due to their own personal limitations, trauma, or lack of trust in people.

This may be a relationship where you are consistently doing the emotional labor to keep the relationship intact. You are the one asking them follow-up questions, asking them how they are doing, prompting them to ask how you are doing, etc. You hope this will help model how they can be emotionally invested in the growth of this relationship, but to no avail.

Sometimes they will overtly tell you that they are emotionally unavailable and that they are aware this is a personal gap area. This admission and self-awareness will make you think that they actually *are* emotionally available, but are simply practicing a moment of self-deprecation.

However, in the words of Maya Angelou, "When someone tells you who they are, believe them."

Sometimes, emotionally unavailable people will start a relationship stating that they like how you push them to be more open and vulnerable. However, those who struggle with emotional availability typically do so for a reason. It is often connected to early trauma, and it feels safer for them to remain closed off.

People who restrict their emotions are usually protecting themselves from past betrayals. Though they may appreciate your support at first, pushing them will eventually be met with resistance and defensiveness. Where it originally felt like healthy, positive growth and enjoyed this part of your relationship, it now becomes overwhelming, leading them to believe that you do not respect their boundaries. They may feel that you are trying to change them and will push back.

Remember, the reasons why a person is emotionally unavailable started long before entering into a relationship with you. Breaking this pattern involves a long-term effort on the part of the unavailable person. They will need to look at the reasons they are restricted in these ways and *then* determine if they even want to change them. This must be a voluntary process led by them and is something that you cannot control.

When it comes to assessing availability, it is important for you to look at what this person is capable of doing right now, in this moment—not the potential of what you or they see as possible.

Is this person capable of living up to their full potential in this moment? Do you feel emotionally seen and understood? There are only two options here: yes or no.

Focusing on the in-between thoughts of "maybe" or "they could be" is what allows us to be in long term, unfulfilling, uneven friendships and relationships. We constantly wait for that one day, which never comes. This *one day* is based on our fantasies of what could be, instead of taking in what the person told us they were available for and what they are actually doing currently.

Inconsistent in their kindness toward you (nice to you in some places but mean to you in others)

In some places, you get a version of them who is very kind, open, and patient with you. They are attentive to your needs, tender, funny, and loving. However, when others come around, their demeanor changes. Where they may have been complimentary before, they are now nitpicky.

Their affection changes to being more physically distant. Their patience and attention for you lessen, and they are aloof to your bids for attention and connection.

This change can happen around select friends, family, exes, potential love rivals, or even the general public. If this person has insisted on keeping your connection a secret, their kindness is reserved for behind closed doors or around certain groups of mutual friends and others.

The back and forth of freely giving and withdrawing kindness when certain people are around is dizzying. But because you have had access to the amazing depth of how loving this person can show up for you *sometimes*, you may be more willing to hold out. You believe they may, with time—after working through whatever their hurdles are—become more consistent.

If this change is taking longer than you wish, you may take an active role in pushing them to be more open via pleas, lectures, threats, and ultimatums.

Public kindness in intimate relationships with healthy and available others is not a privilege or luxury. It is a *basic minimum* standard. If assessing whether someone should be in your inner circle, a consistent level of respect and kindness, in public *and* private, is vital.

Unsupportive of your endeavors

When you share your personal accomplishments and celebrations with this person, they show they are unimpressed and unenthused. There are many ways that one can show their lack of support. Here, we will review: Lack of Acknowledgment, Devil's Advocate, One-Upping, Belittling and Downplaying, Sabotaging, and Being Negative-Focused.

Lack of Acknowledgment

This may be seen overtly in facial expressions or through them quickly changing the subject after a halfhearted acknowledgment.

Sometimes, they won't acknowledge your achievements with positive comments at all, making you wonder if you need to repeat them. Due to their non-response, you may feel the need to push them to react or tell you their thoughts. Similarly, you may get a half-hearted response, a dismissal, or a "Congratulations" that has an edge of bitterness or negativity to it, even if accompanied by a smile.

Devil's Advocate

If they acknowledge your achievement, they may follow up with a devil's advocate point of view of why your good news is not so good. For example:

- "You got a raise, but that just means more taxes."
- "You got a promotion, but wow, that's a lot of stress."
- "You got an interview with a local radio station, but why not the news?"

One-Upping

Some might respond by being competitive, attempting to one-up your achievement with what they are currently working on or have previously done, that is on a higher level. This may be a grander achievement, either real or imagined.

They may over-inflate a previous win or share a triumph that has yet to come to pass, but will be a bigger deal when it occurs. Their goal— to overshadow you.

Belittling and Downplaying

They may belittle your good news by saying your accomplishment or endeavor is great, but one day, you'll have a *real* one.

They may acknowledge your endeavor, but then follow it up with a reminder of how you failed in the past, and highlight your shortcomings. Perhaps they'll remind you how disappointment has previously followed your good news, thus producing anxiety.

This can be poised as them just *looking out for you*, but it ruins your ability to experience your win and be in the moment.

Sabotaging

They may even physically sabotage your upcoming endeavors by physically stopping them. Some examples include:

- dropping out when they said they would help you in a vital role to make your success possible
- causing a competing crisis that happens at the same time as your event
- picking a fight with you right before you're about to engage with your big opportunity, causing you to lose focus
- hiding your keys or returning late with vital items because they *forgot* or *lost track of time*.

Being Negative-Focused

Although they are not interested in talking about the good things that happen, in depth, they can be very open to talking about things that are not going well for you. Here, they want all the details and enjoy commiserating with you, validating how unfair things can be. They may even offer words of encouragement that make you think they are on your side—until you're actually winning.

Again, whether their intention is based on their own pessimistic outlook—they can't help but be negative—or if they wish to intentionally diminish your wins, is unimportant. This differentiation is not a defining factor for availability.

What is most important to identify is whether this person is a safe space for you to share your opportunities and wins. Or do their words and actions always seem to dismantle them? Do you feel compelled to hide or diminish your wins when this person is around? Do you feel dread when the time comes to share this news with them?

Flaky and does not follow through with commitments

They may promise to call you later, show up at your event, help with a needed request, or be available to you. However, something always happens that forces them to bail out. Either there is an emergency that pulls them away, they are feeling emotionally overwhelmed with their own stuff, or they simply change their mind.

An unavailable person who is flaky can sometimes be very apologetic and regretful about letting you down. However, this regret does not result in them changing their behaviors.

For some unavailable people, they may not have any remorse as they feel justified in pulling out. They rationalize their flaky behavior as setting healthy boundaries and implementing self-care.

When assessing for unavailability for someone who consistently lets you down, it does not matter what their intention is. You need to assess whether they really want to be there but can't, or if they are completely indifferent and unremorseful.

You are assessing whether this is someone you can trust to follow-through. Even well-meaning people can sometimes be flaky. They can be quick with promises but unable to keep them.

Acknowledging that does not equate to judging them or calling them bad or selfish people. You are simply making an honest assessment of what they are actually able to give to you at this stage and season in their lives versus what they want to give to you.

Only wants to receive from you, never give

This person is readily available to ask you for advice, for money, for time, for attention, etc. However, they are not as readily available when you need them.

If they do give, it is because you have had to ask for it—sometimes through force and ultimatums or extreme guilting. Rarely do they initiate check-ins, giftings, or favors without expecting you to respond in kind, either immediately or down the road.

Things are often transactional. There is never a free favor or compliment given unless they believe you have generously given the same to them first. They may not hide it, making it clear they are counting the name of fairness. There is no such thing as a free favor as they are used against you or are required to be cashed in at a later date.

Often, their *math* is skewed. It they don't want to do something, they'll find ways to make your requests seem unreasonable, ill-timed, inconvenient, or unfair—regardless of how much you have shown up for them in the past.

Without genuine generosity in a relationship, asking for help becomes stressful. You might fear of punishment, feel pressured to repay favors, or worry being shamed for asking too much.

In these relationships, you are always the giver and often the caretaker.

Sometimes, you may be willing to give this person a pass on their lack of showing up because they are *going through so much.*

However, when it is time to show up for you, it is never a good time for them. They always have a personal crisis with their partner, family, job, or something else where they cannot expend their emotional energy on you.

There is nothing wrong with you choosing to be a supportive friend to a person who is not in a place to give as much as you. These types of relationships can feel rewarding for both sides, especially when this season is temporary. We all need support at times and cannot always be at 100 percent.

However, if this is a persistent pattern, you will often feel drained, underappreciated, neglected, and resentful due to the one-sidedness of this relationship.

They may ghost you when they find something better

This person is readily available for you and a great person to talk to, ask for advice, and have fun—until something better comes along. This may include potential dates, fun opportunities, shopping sales, etc.

This person can be a set of walking contradictions who may give signs of their interest, while also showing they cannot be depended on. Some examples include:

- You have a great time when you're together, and they are always available to hang out until they suddenly disappear, and stop responding because they're in a new relationship
- They have a super engaging conversation with you at a party about all the things you have in common. All the while, they are constantly scanning over your shoulder to see if there is someone more interesting coming in—or then abruptly exit the conversation

- They promise to attend a special event with you, swearing they will make it, until they decide to drop you at the last minute

Sadly, although they will drop you quickly, you may be willing to overlook this because when you're together, it feels *really* good.

Like all items on the unavailability list, we must always use discretion when assessing our relationships.

Is this a pattern where they always (or more often than not) flake out, or was this a onetime occurrence?

If it is the latter, the onetime occurrence may have been hurtful. But, if they have consistently shown up for you elsewhere, this may be an opportunity for you to have a conversation with them for repair and to express your feelings.

However, if you get the sense that you are a placeholder in their life until something better comes along, listen to that voice.

If they are unable or unwilling to follow through, after you communicate your needs for attention and availability to them, this may be a sign this person is unavailable.

Competitive and jealous, one-ups you

With this person, if you have a great story to tell about something that has happened to you, they have a greater one. If you are dating someone new, so are they…and they're cuter. If you have a new promotion, they have a master plan that will bring them a job that's two levels above yours and make them a millionaire.

In your relationship with this person, it feels like they are not genuinely happy for you. Instead, it seems they are engaged in an unspoken competition to beat you. Every time you share something, it is seen as a bid to one-up you instead of being in simple conversation.

This is an issue because those who only know how to be in a competitive stance have an internal need to win at any cost. This means that when a life circumstance or setback happens to you, they may delight in it. They may not directly express this to your face, but they are happy because it means that they can remain Top Dog.

If this is a relationship where the competition is a two-sided healthy battle that is mutually beneficial, then great! Go forth and prosper, as iron sharpens iron!

However, if it is not, they will either root for circumstances that put your emotional, mental, physical, financial, or spiritual self in danger *or* be an active participant in creating the danger.

These are not sources of safety for you, and their attempts to make them your enemy should be acknowledged.

Withholds love and affection, and cuts you off when you set an appropriate boundary

When in a relationship with this person, any attempts to ask for what you need (i.e. more kindness, more attention, more sensitivity, more protection, more financial contribution, etc.) are met with a withdrawal of attention and affection.

This withdrawal is undisguised—you can see it and feel it. It can look like:

- refusals or extreme delays in answering the phone, texts, or other direct messages
- cancelling previously established commitments and dates
- being cold and trying in conversations with you
- refusal to be physically affectionate or keep contact minimal and awkward

You get the sense that they are stonewalling you to punish you and teach you a lesson.

Love addicts sometimes will excuse this withdrawal of affection because they believe that their partner's anger is justified. They wonder if, perhaps; they were at fault, that it is unreasonable or unfair to ask for too much at a time.

However, 9.9999 times out of 10, the request is healthy and appropriate for the relationship to continue. Here are some examples of healthy and appropriate requests:

- be more attentive when in intimate conversations, etc.
- being included in decisions and thought-making processes
- treating you, a child, or someone else with respect
- to be more thoughtful in interactions

Sometimes, the withdrawal is accompanied by an accusation of you being selfish, ungrateful, or not giving them credit for the times they have given you the requested attention, time, and affection. These instances can be fabricated or real. However, upon closer inspection, they may also be examples of them giving you "breadcrumbs" of what you're asking. This is an attempt to lead you to hope that they will, one day, be fully invested in this relationship with you and change.

For someone who is unavailable, the withdrawal may also remain in place even if you backtrack your request(s), apologize, and try to make them feel comfortable.

In healthy relationships, it should always be safe to ask to have your needs met and to be heard without fear of retaliation or retribution. Your needs deserve space as much as the other person's.

You should seek partners who *already* have the tolerance to attend to others' needs without personalizing them as part of their character.

Turning your feelings of hurt from their behaviors back onto you

If the unavailable person is consistently hurting your feelings or the stability of the relationship, you may approach them with a conversation about how this is impacting you.

Even when approached with openness and respect, the unavailable person will turn your experience of feeling harmed back onto you. Instead of looking at how they have hurt you, they reorient the conversation to be about how *they* feel attacked that you feel attacked. You may end up discussing how *they* are harmed by you bringing this up.

They feel as if they have not been given their proper credit; they are being judged, and in fact, *you* are the one who is guilty of being selfish and cold for even suggesting this.

They may speak often in the interaction about it needing to be "fair." To do so, they may bring up incidents that either do not relate to the topic at hand or serve as a great distraction from their own actions.

Their conversation with you about their ownership lacks any validation unless it is the setup to play devil's advocate, i.e., "I can totally get how you would feel that way, but let's say the situation was reversed…[insert way to gaslight you and make the event about them instead of you]."

If they do find the space to listen to your point of view, it is only after you've spent extensive time arguing about why your experience is valid. You've used a large amount of energy to try to prove to them how their actions were hurtful or neglectful. Even if they do concede, you are emotionally exhausted after the exchange.

You are so drained that the validation almost does not feel worth it. This makes you more likely to not bring up the slights in the future because you know each conversation will be so emotionally taxing. Thus, offenses get pushed back and your feelings repressed.

Uses you to emotionally dump their issues

This person is ready and willing to share all their emotional crises with you. You may have initially connected through shared pain, and it seemed that you could understand each other. Or perhaps you came in as the stronger friend or partner, able to see the potential in this amazing person that they could not see in themselves. You held their hand through many an obstacle and proved your loyalty.

This fidelity is an awesome show of your character, but it also makes it difficult for you to create boundaries. You started off as an emotional shoulder to cry on, thus you may question if you have a right to pull back, without abandoning them. However, what you do know is that their constant shares are starting to overwhelm and drain you, emotionally.

Another possibility is this person may dominate your catch-up times with stories about themselves, asking you for feedback and support. There is very little time spent on what you need or want to discuss.

Using friends and loved ones for emotional support and feedback is one of the benefits of intimate relationships. However, this shifts into an unavailable relationship when there is no space for you to share what *you* need. Here are some examples of what this can look like:

- They do not have time to listen to you or learn your full story
- They give halfhearted responses and follow-up questions—if any at all—when you share
- They do not initiate asking about you and how you're doing
- They do not inquire or follow up on things you have shared with them before
- They only seem to be available to you when *they* are in need of a crisis buddy. However, in times of calm, happiness, and relationship bliss, they are nowhere to be found
- When you do get to talk, they rush through your part of the conversation

If you mention how this is hurtful or that you feel crowded out, they may become either defensive or super apologetic.

They may react in two ways:

Their response might be defensive and they will claim to be too overwhelmed to listen and lack the energy to support you because they feel attacked by you. They might justify their self focus or directly state they are unable to support you emotionally at the moment.

If their response is apologetic, they will apologize with promises to improve. They may even do better, briefly. Soon, old habits take over and conversations will return to being focused only on their needs.

Crowds you out and only focuses on themselves

When it is time to check in, they spend most of the time talking about themselves and their updates. They tell long stories and may ask for your opinion and thoughts, but leave little space for you to insert your thoughts and experiences. When you do, they bring the topic back to themselves, how the situation affects them, triggers they may have, or experiences that center around them as the main character.

Sometimes, you may feel as if you are just there as an audience member, not a participant in the conversation.

When it is time for you to talk about yourself, if not being self-focused, they may:

- Shortly end the conversation because now they have to go
- Giving short, non-responses to your stories that do not have follow-up questions and statements

If you mention that you feel like you do not have a space to share, they may:

- Get super defensive and say they feel attacked
- Make an apology and promise to do better

However, the unavailable person will be unable to follow through with their promise to be equitable in your conversations.

They may make a few attempts, but your conversations will eventually return to being focused on them, with them rarely (or never) meaningfully asking you how you're doing and taking the space and time to listen.

Controlling

Your moments together are defined by what they want and the timeline they want it to be accomplished in. Whether it's the restaurant you prefer, when you will meet, or even how you communicate, they need to be in control and have the final say.

When you attempt to make your thoughts known, they find fault with your opinions and share openly why they won't work. In moments of conflict, the focus is on how the perceived slight has affected them emotionally. They need to be emotionally calmed by you—validated and soothed before they can consider your point of view.

Sometimes, their consideration is still unsatisfying as they do not seem to fully understand the impact of their behavior on your feelings. They may offer a half-hearted apology or what appears to be a genuine apology. They may promise that they will be better about sharing space and compromising in the future. However, this does not happen unless accompanied by sabotaging what you were asking for or using their concession against you later.

When you're on the receiving end of this for a long time, even the most resolved people can get worn down. They find it easier to just go along with what the person wants rather than continue to fight constantly.

Excludes and leaves you out

When they have an event or a special occasion to celebrate, sometimes you are invited, and sometimes you are not. You may hear about private hangouts from mutual friends that you were unaware of.

There may have been times when you were invited, but it felt as if they were doing so out of obligation, either because of your mutual connections or because they knew you might find out.

If they attend your events, they may not stay for long, or they may say they are coming and then bail out at the last moment. You cannot shake this nagging feeling that you are not a valued member of their circle, even if you consider them to be a part of yours.

Feels entitled to your resources and attention/expects you to give

They are upset when you say you are unavailable to share your time, resources, money, or affection in the exact moments and depth they need it. They expect you to be available for their support. Anything other than an immediate agreement is seen as a betrayal.

You are made to feel guilty for having boundaries. If they fail or have hurdles, you are either directly or passively blamed for why it did not work out for them. At times, you have enjoyed the feeling of being needed and helping them, but it has become a never-ending pattern of requests.

With them, there is no accounting for the countless times before when you have shown up for them. Every new perceived slight erases any goodwill you have previously given them. They are not satisfied until you give your all, and even then, it's not enough. They still need more.

Is emotionally draining to be around

These folks are always amid a crisis and want to use you for the mental and emotional support needed to get through. You are a resource rather than a friend. Whether they make the conversation all about themselves or ask for a favor, being in a relationship with them is like you are a 911 operator without the training and the mental health benefits.

You may find that the good times are no longer as redeeming as they used to be and you may feel dread when you see their name in your notifications.

Whether it is emotionally, mentally, spiritually, financially, or physically, in these relationships, you are always the one giving more than they are. They are either not interested, don't know how to, or are incapable of matching your energy due to their own status in life.

Saying a person doesn't have the capacity to match your energy is *not* being judgmental. If anything, it can be the most loving and honest commentary. Especially if you are acknowledging how and where this person can be emotionally blocked and unable to show up.

In actuality, the worst and most unloving thing is to ask someone to be something they are not and not meet them where they are.

True love chooses someone where they currently are in that moment. If what they have for you does not fit your needs, it is okay to admit it. From there, you can either adjust your expectations of the relationship or create space as needed.

Disinterested in you and/or seems to just tolerate you

They have either directly told you or you have a nagging sense that they do not truly enjoy you as a person. At times, you may wonder if they even like you.

When you spend time with them together, they may appear distracted, disinterested, or "half there," in some way. They may be rushing to the next thing or not seemingly interested in what you have to say.

Even if you are physically in the same household, share a business, have children, or regularly work together in some capacity, you have wondered if they may be there either out of convenience or obligation due to their lack of effort.

This disinterest usually is accompanied by some form of neglect of your needs. Whether they are your emotional needs by not being interested in how you're doing or supportive needs by not following up when asked to show up for you. There is a felt sense that they can't be bothered with you, and this felt sense happens more often than not.

If they do show up for you, it is after multiple reminders and pushing on your end. They are often more focused on their needs and how to get what they want before considering yours.

Chapter 9:
Special Considerations

As we know, the world is not all black and white. There are nuances between people, relationships, their preferences, and what their capacity to show up means.

Though it is impossible to detail every single nuance, I have selected a few common situations that may be important to consider when assessing if a person is truly available or unavailable.

A temporary life stage transition and/or changes in capacity

Life can come at you fast and force you into transition. Some transitions require intense focus and concentration. They take us from our normal routines and relationships to one where we cannot show up and perform we did before.

If you have a friend or have been the person who has been in one of these life transitions, you may have seen this first hand. The person in this position may have been previously available is now unable to be as consistent as they were before.

Perhaps they lost a loved one and are now grieving? Are they become the primary caretaker to aging parents or have they received a cancer diagnosis? Perhaps they are experiencing job loss and must now be more conservative with time and finances? Or are they new parents or stepparents to minor children?

There are countless situations that may make a person who was a stable and consistent presence in our lives no longer be able to show up in the way they were before.

If you have a loved one in this stage, it is up to you to decide if this is:

1) a relationship that you can remain supportive of with their current capacity

and

2) a relationship you are willing to adjust your expectations for due to their life stage transition?

As shared in this guide, though you may have empathy, your needs are still important. Should you decide to adjust your expectations for your friend, your need for companionship and care does not disappear. It is still important that you are intentionally looking for other sources to have your needs met so that you do feel any disappointment and/or resentment for how this person is currently showing up.

Neurodivergent conditions

Neurodivergent people have brains that process information differently than neurotypical people. Neurodivergent disorders include Autism Spectrum Disorder (ASD), Attention Deficit Hyperactivity Disorder (ADHD), Dyslexia, Obsessive Compulsive Disorder, and more.

While symptomology varies between each, these conditions can result in many ways. Differences in communication styles, executive functioning (i.e. time and organization skills), learning styles, sensory sensitivities, mental functioning, difficulties with emotion regulation are just a few.

If you are in a relationship with a neurodivergent person, what this means for you is that they may absolutely be doing their best to be available to you. However, due to their neural networking, they may:

- Not be able to fully communicate their emotions and thoughts to your desired level
- Have a high emotional sensitivity or feel frequently overwhelmed
- Struggle with maintaining consistency in a relationship
- Battle with timeliness and organization
- Rely on strict routines and schedules to maintain stable functionality, which may impact their flexibility
- Need more time to withdraw and recharge to decompress and get grounded

For example, if the person has symptoms of ADHD, time blindness is a real symptom of the disorder. Thus, despite intentional attempts and proactive planning, your partner may still struggle with consistent lateness and missing deadlines. These errors truly have nothing to do with whether they value you or not. Their brain simply works differently, and while medication may help, it is not a cure-all.

If your partner has symptoms of Autism Spectrum Disorder, this may impact their ability to understand the emotional consequences of their communication, especially if it skews towards being more direct and unfiltered. They may also struggle with being able to wholly explain what they are feeling in the moment. They may need more space, guidance, or openness on your part to understand *their* way of communicating their needs.

With that said, it is completely up to you to decide what this means for your relationship. Are you willing to adjust your expectations, knowing that this is an unintentional impact of their neurodivergence? Or do you create space to adjust the level of intimacy and reliance you have on them?

There is no right answer here. You know what you need most in your closest intimate relationships, to feel safe and supported. However, it is important to factor this, if it applies, into your next steps.

If this is a person you would like to keep in your life, you will need to spend intentional time learning about their condition. And, would be helpful to learn how to be supportive in a healthy relationship with them.

Has an <u>untreated </u>addiction or mental disorder

Much like the neurodivergent conditions listed above, mental illnesses and addictions in and of themselves are not red flags of unavailability.

Millions of people around the world battle with a variety of mental health disorders and/or addictions, every day. Many reading this guide will have their own diagnoses as well including but not limited to those such as Generalized Anxiety Disorder and Depression.

However, for the sake of this guide, we are focusing on the long-term impact of dealing with someone whose addiction and/or mental disorder is **both** untreated and unmanaged.

For the person struggling with an untreated addiction or mental health disorder, no matter how much they may want to show up for you, their condition *will* impact their functioning and ability to show up.

Unfortunately, untreated and undiagnosed mental disorders may place you in harm's way as a partner, family member, or friend. You may expend countless hours, energy, and resources trying to help whether it is physically, emotionally, mentally, financially, or even legally. However, in these cases, more intervention is needed than what you are able to give especially if you are the only one putting in the work to find solutions.

Many love addicts, especially if there is a history of addiction in their family or community, may instinctively end up overextending and trying to help their loved "fix" these issues. They are used to stepping in as caretakers for others as this may have been their role in childhood and previous relationships.

However, if the person on the receiving end is struggling and does not want help or seems to always sabotage and not follow through with presented solutions, you are recreating your previous trauma of trying to help someone recover that is beyond your scope of control. Though earlier trauma may have taught you otherwise, it has **never** been your responsibility to save someone who is not willing or open to receive help.

If you choose not to help this person in the ways you used to overextend in the past, know that it is possible to be a kind and loving person who sees the best and potential in everyone and still be protective of your own mental and emotional health.

It is okay to be a supportive ear to those who need it, but prioritize relationships that are mutually beneficial to you, are super easy and pleasurable. It is okay to recognize that some relationships require more than you are able to give, especially if they are unwilling to receive it. You do not need to sacrifice yourself to prove you are a good daughter, sister, wife, partner, or friend.

Self-Assessment Questions

- Do you have any relationships that fall under these special circumstances?
- Has learning about the nuance of these special circumstances adjusted your feelings about these relationships in any way? If yes, how so?
- Are these relationships that you feel you will be able to keep as is or are changes you may need to make?
- If making personal changes, list the names of the people below and what changes you will be making on your end for the relationship

Person's Name	Special Circumstance(s)	Changes I Will Make

Chapter 10:
The Availability Scale for Relationships

As shared previously in this guide, the list of Availability Qualities versus Unavailability Qualities is <u>not</u> a "Pros and Cons" list.

The items on the availability list are integral components to a safe and healthy relationship. Without them present, you will feel depleted emotionally, mentally, socially, spiritually, and financially.

The unavailability list includes qualities that are emotionally, mentally, and spiritually dangerous, harmful, and abusive. As such, they should treated as bright warning signs of danger.

For this reason, it is encouraged that for each important relationship in your life, that you rate each partnership according to The Availability Scale for Relationships ©.

- - -

How to Use The Availability Scale for Relationships ©

For each of your primary relationships, grab a sheet of paper and title it with their name. Underneath their name, for every availability characteristic, give the person +10 points. For every sign of unavailability, give them -50 points. Add up the points each relationship in total.

Using the Availability Scale, there are 7 levels Availability:
1. Best Friend, Lover, & Partner (BLP) Availability
2. Good Friend Availability
3. Associate Availability
4. Casual Acquaintanceship Availability
5. Stranger Danger Availability
6. Extremely Dangerous Availability
7. Critically Dangerous Availability

Using the point scale below, determine where each of your relationships fall in levels of availability.

See our companion workbook, "How to Pick Partners for Love Addicts Workbook," for detailed worksheets to rate and determine next steps for each of your relationships.

A Note About New Relationships

Before you jump into rating your relationships, understand that for newer relationships, they may begin on the lower scale as you are just getting to know them. It may take time for you to see markers of availability and unavailability.

It is okay to go slow in the get to know you process. There is no rush. However, what is most important is that you pay attention to both green flags and red flags as you observe them and rate them accordingly.

The Availability Scale for Relationships ©

200 pts - Best Friend, Lover, & Partner (BLP) Availability

This person meets all the markers of availability and is an excellent candidate to be a best friend, a lover, or partner in some capacity. You can trust they will be open and honest and care about your experience as well.

From here, you are free to assess for compatibility and if you would like to build a connection long term. It is possible that you meet someone who has these incredible qualities, but you are not a good fit in values, common interests, or in what you want long-term.

For those where there is shared compatibility on shared interests, values and long-term goals, these qualities will not prevent you from having to put effort into this relationship.

The presence of these qualities do not mean you will not ever have miscommunications and disagreements. Rather, it does mean that when this occurs, you both will have the skillsets and emotional maturity to work through conflicts and grow together.

150 to 199 pts - Good Friend Availability

At the level of Good Friend, they are someone you may spend time with often and share parts of your life with. However, they may not be someone you do so with consistently. This person meets most of the markers of availability and shows they have a genuine interest in your well-being and showing up for the relationship.

Depending on the availability markers that are not present, you can decide if this is a relationship you would like to invest in more to see if the markers may be reciprocated on their side as well or leave them as a good friend.

100 to 149 pts - Associate Availability

At an Associate level, you may have shared activities and hobbies (i.e. a sports league, a coworking relationship, dance class, etc) where you work together in some capacity. You are most likely cordial but there is no real investment in getting to know you and pursuing a relationship.

If you have known this person for some time and/or may an attempt to get to know them and the effort has not been reciprocated, it may be best to leave this relationship where it is as this person is either most likely not interested in moving forward or may not have the capacity to do so.

50 to 99 pts - Casual Acquaintance Availability

Similar to the Associate level of availability, you may be cordial or have polite interactions, but this isn't someone who is available to move forward with in an intimate relationship. Either they have shown low interest in investing in the relationship **or** they show up to multiple signs of unavailability even if there are signs of availability present.

As a reminder, signs of unavailability are not simple quirks but relationship (and self esteem) destroying behaviors. The presence of multiple signs of unavailability would completely offset the benefits found in the relationship at this level.

If choosing to keep this relationship based on the other available benefits, it is best to keep this relationship purely at a casual acquaintance level. This will help you lesson the effects of being on the receiving end of the consequences of unavailable behaviors and prevent you from attempting to invest in a relationships that is not mutual.

However, should you start to see a change in their signs of unavailability over time that is led and internally motivated by them, you may reassess in the future.

49 to -100 pts - Stranger Danger Availability

At this level, if you believe you are close with this person, there may be elements of deception in this relationship due to the multiple signs of unavailability needed to make this score set. Thus, the title "Stranger" is appropriate. Though you may be intimately connected with them, you may not really know them at all.

Even if there are signs of availability, with multiple signs of unavailability present, there is a high probability that this person is breadcrumbing and masking to get what they want from you.

Possibilities of what they could want include proximity to your status and energy, financial resources, emotional support, sexual contact and intimacy, entertainment, temporary companionship, caretaking and domestic support, career advancement and advice, and much more.

The breadcrumbing and masking are not always done maliciously. While there are some people who are intentionally predatory, some are unaware of how their distancing techniques affect others and the relationship.

However, at this level, one should not excuse any signs of unavailability as being solely based on ignorance. Even if not malicious in intent, this person is still intentionally keeping your relationship superficial at best and transactional to their benefit at worst. They are not showing up with full emotional honesty and transparency.

Should you have someone in your life that rates at this level, it is important to pay attention to where and how they show up consistently in your life. Are you magnifying moments of kindness based on what you would like to see versus what proceeds and surrounds those events? Are they disappointing you consistently more often than them showing up fully?

-101 to -500 - Extremely Dangerous Unavailability

At this level, this personal marks anywhere between 3 and 11 markers of unavailability.

No matter what their words say, this person shows very clearly with their actions that they do not mean to protect you. In many cases, they may not like you very much as well.

To stay in connection with this person means you will have continual moments of felt rejection and/or abandonment. Depending on your trauma patterns, you will be susceptible to personalizing to believe that they are acting this way because:

- You have failed in some way, are inadequate or are not good enough
- You just need to be more patient, more merciful, and gracious while they are working through their faults
- You are asking for too much and if you were more confident and self-assured, you wouldn't be hurt by their actions because you wouldn't be so "needy"

None of these thoughts are ever the case. As shared multiple times in this guide, you are worthy of the love, kindness, fidelity, and attention you desire.

All markers in the Available qualities list are **basic** standards for anyone you choose to have in your inner circle. However, even for those who are not in your inner circle, they are basic standards of kindness and respect needed for *any person* to have access to you in any form of relationship.

At the Extremely Dangerous Unavailability level, this relationship is, at best, very emotionally neglectful and, at worst, mentally and emotionally abusive.

Though this relationship does not meet the point levels for the "Critically Dangerous Unavailability" level below, it is still strongly suggested you read that section as well to see the long-term effects of staying this this type of relationship.

-500 to -1000 pts - Critically Dangerous Unavailability

This person marks nearly every marker on the Signs of Unavailability checklist. If you stay in relationship with this person, you will not only be at risk of emotional and mental abuse while in the partnership but having to work through the residual trauma once you leave. The effects of staying these types of relationships include but are not limited to:

- lowered self-esteem,
- emotional trauma,
- medical and somatic issues (due to the stress on your body),
- negative impact on your relationships with others
- depression and loss of interest
- isolation and exclusion
- loss of voice and sense of empowerment
- extreme fatigue
- vocational issues
- financial issues

When one finds out they have been in a relationship of this nature, it is tempting to resign to staying in it. You may:

- Personalize blame for being here: "I saw the signs. I should've known better. I deserve this"
- Believe that it is impossible or too much work to leave ("I'm already here now. I'm too tired to figure this out. I'll try to make the best of it or stand up for myself more.")

Neither lines of thought here are true. The person who is to blame for the mental, emotional, and spiritual abuse in this relationship is the other person, **not you**.

Also, attempting to stand up for yourself in a relationship of this level is impossibly hard as the relationship has been built on 1) the slow dismantlement of your voice and connection to your personal power and 2) the other's person general disinterest in your well-being unless it benefits them. There are no words or actions you can say that will be able to successfully force, cajole, or convince this person to comply with what you are asking nor feel empathy for the impact of their actions on your sense of self worth.

At this level, this person is more focused on their own self-interest and what benefits them. No matter the words, declarations of love, apologies, or promises they give, their history of actions speaks for itself.

Know that <u>at **any** time you can leave and decide this is not working for you anymore</u> – whether you have invested 4 days or 4 decades. Whether you have a shared business together or shared children. Whether you have left 6 times already and came back the first five. It is **NEVER** too late. You need a healthy you to show up for your business, for your children, and most importantly – yourself.

The impact of the abuse of this relationship has made you think that you waited too long, that you're too old, that you would look too silly, or you would hurt too many people to leave. This is all untrue.

Your self-esteem and self- empowerment will immediately improve once you are not connected to this person. You are worthy of feeling that good. It does get to be easier. Your proximity and consistent communication has made you doubt your worth.

The process of leaving a toxic trauma bonded relationship can be very hard. It is not as simply as just "doing it." Had it been, you would've done it by now.

If you need support ending this relationship, check out my book, "The No Contact Guide for Love Addicts" for a step by step process on creating distance with toxic relationships while healing within.

Chapter 11:
Putting the Focus on You

In addition to assessing your current relationships, use this guide to illuminate the places *you* might benefit to grow.

For each of your primary relationships, use the Availability vs. Unavailability Qualities Chart and mark which qualities you exhibit in your relationship with them. You may find that you have more of one set of qualities in some relationships than others. You may find some areas that you would like to double down on and do more of, and others you would like to heal and change.

Personal growth and self-accountability are important qualities needed to maintain every healthy relationship.

In a journal or another writing surface, use the following questions to help guide you on the next steps you would like to take:

- "What qualities of Availability that I currently do well in, are the ones I want to keep doing?
- "Which qualities of Availability do I want to grow in?"

- "Which qualities of Unavailability do I lean towards in friendships and relationships? Would I like to challenge them or keep doing them?"
- "Does my availability change depending on who is around me? If yes, how so?"
- "Are there available people I have been pushing away who could offer safer relationships? If yes, how will I move closer to them?"
- "Are there any unavailable people I need to create distance with? If yes, how will I do so?"

Besides these questions of self-reflection, therapy can be helpful to determine the root causes of why the way you show up within your relationships and how each one may differ. We often have underlying patterns that are created from our past experiences and unresolved trauma. These patterns are often learned which means they can be unlearned too, which is great news for those who want healthy, thriving relationships.

Part 3:
Applying this Information to Your Relationships

Chapter 12: Reassessing Your Relationships

Now, let's reassess the top three relationships you mentioned at the beginning of this guide and see if your answers have changed.

Assess Your Relationships

On a scale of 0 to 5, where would you rank your primary loved ones as far as their availability to attend to your emotional needs, to be of support, and to be physically available?

Then answer the questions below. Assess why you gave this ranking, the ways this relationship benefits or challenges you, and whether you should want to keep this relationship as is or change it. You may use another sheet of paper to write your answers if needed.

Relationship #1: _____

1	2	3	4	5
Unavailable				Available

How did my ranking change, if at all, after reading Parts 1 and 2 of this book?

Are there any new ways I have learned this relationship benefits me?

Are there any new ways I have learned this relationship harms me?

Am I showing up as available or unavailable to them?

Are there any ways I would like to change how I show up in this relationship?

Would I like to move closer to this person, keep it the same, or create distance?

Relationship #2: _____

1	2	3	4	5
Unavailable				Available

How did my ranking change, if at all, after reading this book?

Are there any new ways I have learned this relationship benefits me?

Are there any new ways I have learned this relationship harms me?

Am I showing up as available or unavailable to them?

Are there any ways I would like to change how I show up in this relationship?

Would I like to move closer to this person, keep it the same, or create distance?

Relationship #3: _____

1	2	3	4	5
Unavailable				Available

How did my ranking change, if at all, after reading this book?

Are there any new ways I have learned this relationship benefits me?

Are there any new ways I have learned this relationship harms me?

Am I showing up as available or unavailable to them?

Are there any ways I would like to change how I show up in this relationship?

Would I like to move closer to this person, keep it the same, or create distance?

Being clear about how you see each of your relationships—what is working and what is not—is the first step in gaining clarity on whether it is meeting your emotional, mental, and relational needs.

Now let's look at how to apply what you have learned.

Chapter 13:
When They're Available

When you find a friend, loved one, or partner, what does that mean? How do you move forward?

For love addicts, their greatest desire is to love and to be loved, but usually have a long history of choosing unavailable people. They make them do all the emotional labor and are so consumed with their own personal needs; they do not get to know the hearts, wants, and desires of the love addict.

Available relationships are different. This person is not only bringing their full self, which includes their needs, opinions, and boundaries. They are open to learning about the needs, wants, and hopes of the love addict. They want to see them on their best days *and* their worst days. There is authenticity in their connection that requires no payment in return for their love and loyalty. There is no need for competition, one-upping, nor living on the defensive with them. It's easy…. Almost *too* easy, the love addict may think.

Years of trauma have taught them that when things are *too good*, then there is impending danger on the horizon. And if there is not, they can create a crisis or sabotage the connection by creating some unavailable habits of their own.

If this is you, no worries. This is normal. Your nervous system has long equated intimacy with the need to fight, flee, or freeze because of the impending danger. Just because you are in a safe location does not mean that your body, mind, and soul believe it.

This is where doing internal work, therapy, and somatic practices will help you to relieve the trauma that created these ingrained fears. Thankfully, you were not born with these patterns. They were learned over years of disappointment, neglect, and betrayals in your relationships. But luckily, because they were learned, they can be unlearned as well.

For those who may be experiencing available relationships for the first time, here are four ways for you to cultivate these relationships rather than push them away.

Tip 1: Feel comfortable initiating quality time with them

It is totally okay for you to initiate quality time with this person. Whether it is a catch-up phone call, a dinner date, or hanging out in the park with your kids, you can initiate a time to get together rather than waiting for them to do so first.

Be mindful that, especially as adults, not being immediately available for your first invitation does not equally mean that they are uninterested or unavailable. Busy schedules are the norm for most adults. Even the most willing persons may need to schedule new friend dates out a bit.

If feeling triggered by the time and space in between, pay close attention to if this is related to wounds from previous people who were unavailable to you. What stories did that trauma tell you about your worth or what happens with other people when you let them in? Can you do some healing work to rewrite these stories and see these pending friend dates from a more neutral perspective?

Love and intimacy are built over time. This can be in contrast to the whirlwind connection patterns that love addicts are used to. In the past, they may have been guided by intense feelings that are quickly and aggressively reciprocated. That led to either a deeply entrenched romance or fast best friends. However, without having a firm foundation to grow on, often, these types of relationships either fizzle out over time, or crash and burn with the same intensity they started with.

Love addicts must learn that it is okay to go slow, to take one's time. That their worth and safety are not determined by the speed at which this relationship grows, but by how they feel about themselves in the process.

With that said, feel comfortable initiating friend dates. Don't wait for them to do it all the time and conjure stories about why they haven't. Sometimes, what we can perceive as flakiness or disinterest can be our reflexive response to perceived threats of abandonment and rejection. So, we are try to cut them off before they can harm us—even if the fear is purely internal, and a person has given us no indication that a threat is imminent.

Tip 2: Feel comfortable initiating vulnerable feelings and shares with them

It is safe to share with this person your thoughts, feelings, dreams, desires, and wants. They will even want to listen to your complaints, rants, and your venting sessions. This person wants to hear it all.

They are available to you because they are interested in *you*. This includes what makes you tick, what makes you laugh, what makes you cry, and even what makes you want to burst out in song. If they did not care about you, they wouldn't be there or be showing these signs of availability.

Love addicts often feel they must censor who they are and their expression for fear of being too much. They fear that if they showed *all* of who they are, the person would get scared away.

As a result, they often believe they must piecemeal themselves out to not overwhelm and scare people off. The inner fears are:

- "No one cares about what I'm feeling,"
- "My thoughts, who I am, is a burden,"
- "I am too much/I need too much."

So, they hide and never truly allow themselves to share or be vulnerable with the available person.

However, your loved ones want to get to know you and your thoughts. If this is hard to believe, consider how deeply *you* want to get to know your loved ones. You have a deep curiosity about their thoughts and motivations. You want to know how you can make them happy and take delight in being that person for them. Well, the available person feels the same about you.

You are worth that type of love and consideration.

This may be hard to believe, not just because of previous trauma that you've been through, but because *you* believe those things about yourself. So even when you have others who make space for you in conversation, inquire how you're doing, and express interest in what makes you tick, your internal filter says:

- "No, they don't really mean that."
- "No, they're just being nice."
- "No, I really don't have anything interesting to say or share anyway."

Though you have said you're tired of relationships that neglect you, it becomes so much easier to become needless and wantless because you get to hide.

That is why it is so important for you to do the internal work, to become more available to others by way of becoming available to yourself.

To do this, you must learn to like *and* enjoy yourself. Enjoy your thoughts, emotions, dreams, and desires, and be shameless about sharing them with the available and safe people in your life. To get there, you must first believe you are worth seeing and valuing as a prize.

Tip 3: Feel comfortable inviting them to be a part of your life and day

One of the first tasks I have for my clients who struggle with intimacy and pushing people away is to learn how to invite people in daily.

This involves proactively sharing your goings-on as they are occurring—not weeks later—checking in with them just to say hi, remembering what is going on with them, and then following up.

When in a relationship with unavailable people, love addicts struggle to not overshare and enmesh their partner in everything. However, with available and healthy people, sharing becomes burdensome, annoying, and unnecessary. The deep desire to spend time with and get to know someone is now replaced with fears of being too much and overwhelming them. Or perhaps it's replaced with newfound secrecy, where they don't want to share their goings-on with someone because it's not their business.

It is important for the love addict to move closer to these safe relationships, while doing their own internal work to face the triggers of trauma, rejection, and insecurities that may come up. This will allow them to enjoy healthy love and relationships without reverting to old patterns of protecting themselves from true intimacy.

They must learn what it is like to be seen in relationships with available people versus chasing the attention and acceptance of those who are unavailable. They must also learn that it is possible to maintain their individuality while still being vulnerable.

Letting the *right* people in only benefits and enhances the beautiful life you have cultivated, not detracts.

Tip 4: Make amends (apologize) when you notice you are sabotaging and then do something different

If this is your first time being in an available relationship or partnership, you will undoubtedly make mistakes.

As a love addict, close relationships can be triggering when you first enter them. As you reflect, you might notice ways you've unintentionally created distance or sabotaged relationships through your own unavailability.

There are a variety of ways this occurs, but here are some common examples:

- Picking fights out of nowhere, including zeroing in on phrases if not said the exact way you want to hear them, even though you know the intent
- Getting busy and creating distance by deliberately picking up work commitments
- Attempting to break up
- Inviting other parties into the relationship by intentionally hanging out with other friends to diffuse the time you spend with them
- Small, harmless quirks start to feel increasingly irritating
- Projecting past betrayals onto them, making them pay for your previous traumas by expecting them to tolerate your accusations and harmful behavior

To repair the relationship, we may need to apologize and make amends. We must learn that just because have met the *right* person for us, this love does not erase the impact of our previous fears and traumas.

We have most likely built incomplete communication patterns and have had poor models of what healthy partnership and friendship look like. When we meet these people, we will still have years' worth of defense mechanisms, insecurities, and fears of harm that we must unlearn.

What a healthy friendship or partnership gives us is a safe place to work through these wounds versus being the full answer to these experiences. We still must do the work of recognizing when we are:

- projecting our trauma on the other person,
- attempting to flee because it's getting too real and too vulnerable,
- afraid of losing our individuality and independence
- creating problems when none exist
- proactively trying to reject the other person before they reject us
- requesting the other person to fix a deeply embedded inner child wound that existed before them

In my online coaching program, The Love Addiction Recovery School, I have helped hundreds of women unravel the sources of these traumas and relearn healthy relationship skills to help them cultivate and maintain the relationships of their dreams. Using my therapeutic background, I've created practical and applicable lessons women can use in their everyday life to unlearn the effects of love addiction, love avoidance, and the trauma that causes it to improve their relationships with themselves and others.

You can learn more or join by visiting: therecoveryschool.com

We will talk more about what apologies may look like in the "Communication" chapter of this book. However, for now, let's look at what we can do if we find this person is unavailable for us.

Self-Assessment Questions

- Which of the four tips for being available do you find the easiest? Why?
- Which of the four tips for being available do you find the most difficult? Why?
- What support do you think you may need to cultivate being more available?

Chapter 14:
When They're Unavailable

So, you have assessed the person, and according to the guide, they are unavailable. Now what? Do you cut them off? Do you downgrade the relationship? Do you have to start all over?

Human relationships are full of nuances and are rarely black and white. In this chapter, we will review how to evaluate relationships where someone's availability doesn't quite match your needs, but the connection is still healthy. We'll also explore what steps to take when someone's unavailability is part of a larger pattern that negatively impacts your daily life.

When They're Unavailable, but They're Not Problematic

In this section, we will review ways a relationship may be unavailable, but the nuances of the relationship are not harmful to our everyday life.

Their unavailability is temporary and/or circumstantial

Sometimes, we may find some people who are typically very healthy for us. But due to current life circumstances or lack of capacity, they are unavailable. This qualifies as someone who has shown up consistently for you in all areas in the past, but due to these special circumstances, they are limited.

For example, say you are close friends with a new mother. She has been your closest friend for years; you know that she understands you better than everyone else and vice versa. You have both equally given all of yourselves through kindness, love, and healthy sacrificial bonds throughout your friendship. However, with her having a newborn child, her capacity to show up in the same way as before has either decreased drastically or changed completely.

Even with the best of support and help, her emotional capacity has been split, and her physical health and energy levels to show up for you physically, have been impacted as well.

Thus, your friend is still the same woman you originally connected with. You may even love her more now at this stage of her life. However, she may not be able to attend every social gathering or be completely awake during a catch-up conversation. But she still cares and supports you in spirit.

This is where it is good to practice our own self-reflection and self-regulation. As an available and supportive friend, maybe it is best for you to learn about what she needs during this time to show up for her as support. Instead of expecting a 50/50 split in effort, perhaps this life stage requires a 70/30 or 80/20 split. Perhaps this would help you negotiate the new normal of this friendship and/or reduce your expectations in certain areas during this season in her life.

However, your personal needs for community and emotional support have not disappeared because your friend is transitioning to a new life stage. Thus, knowing that she is not currently available, you are intentional about getting your needs for quality time met via other friendships and social events.

You must not ever go without fulfilling your own needs. Waiting for a partner or another person to fulfill them—this dependence can easily produce undue resentment. You are the one who is in charge of getting your needs met and if you are in a place of self-neglect waiting for the other; it puts you both in a compromising and unfair position.

Unavailability does not mean that you must go into no contact

Just because you discover that someone is unavailable to your needs does not mean that you must have no contact with them or cut them off.

It is very common—especially if you battle with an intimacy disorder like love addiction or love avoidance—to think in terms of black-and-white absolutes when it comes to relationships. For example:

- Either we're together, or I never talk to you again
- Either you're my best friend, or I treat you like a stranger on the street
- Either I can tell you everything, or I tell you nothing

The truth is that this guide is simply a source of information for you to determine what your rules of engagement will be when it comes to certain relationships.

What is it that someone needs to present for you to 1) let them into your life and 2) at which level of intimacy?

The problem is often that many only have the two black and white categories—all in or completely out—without realizing that there is a whole spectrum of levels for connection.

You may find that someone you considered a good friend is not meeting you with the same energy. You have already had a conversation with them about this and expressed your needs and requests for change. (See the chapter on "Communication" for more information on how this may look).

Unfortunately, nothing has changed. So now you have an opportunity to adjust the relationship level. However, there are many levels between "Best Friend Forever" and "Someone I Used to Know."

Here are some examples of relationship levels you may have:

> Life Partner/Committed Partner
> Best friend
> Close friend
> Casual friend
> Mutual associate
> Colleague
> Stranger
> Frenemy/enemy
> Predator/unsafe person

Each of these types of relationships will have different levels of access to your time, your emotions, your inner thoughts, life, affection, and resources.

In this scenario, you get to decide if you are downgrading a best friend to someone who is a close friend, casual friend, or even a colleague. You also get to decide if someone you had as a casual friend needs to be relabeled to be an unsafe person/predator with whom you need to cut off contact.

Remember, the signs of unavailability are not just cons, but actions that can cause you emotional, mental, physical, financial, spiritual, or sexual harm. This includes if the person is in the category of "Life Partner/Committed Partner." In these relationships, it is even more important that we do not ignore the red flags, as their behavior impacts even more facets of our lives.

If someone shows you who they are, believe them and label them appropriately.

Labeling them as unavailable does not make you mean or judgmental

Two things can be true at the same time:

> Truth #1: Someone is a great person who is doing their best. They are honestly putting in their best effort. However, they have gone through many things that have made their capacity to show up less than ideal for themselves and others.

> and

> Truth #2: This person's limited capacity may be overwhelming, draining, and detrimental to you mentally, emotionally, physically, financially, and even spiritually.

Many of us who were groomed to be codependent have a knee-jerk reaction to rescue someone if we see them in pain—even if their actions are simultaneously hurting us, as well.

We may turn a blind eye to how their actions affect our lives because we feel responsible for prioritizing fixing them and being fair to them. For us to be good, kind, empathic people, we are not allowed to be mean, which means practicing honesty and clarity about where someone is.

The most loving thing you can do for *any* person is to see them for exactly who and where they are. The assessment of their capacity, strengths and flaws is a neutral and honest process.

From there, determine how you are available to interact with them from there. It is unloving to see someone as who you want them to be and then attempt to mold, manipulate, or coerce them to change.

"Everyone has flaws. Everyone is human. Who am I to judge?"

This is absolutely true. You will not find any person who is blameless and faultless in *any* relationship 100% of the time.

This availability guide is not about holding others (and yourself) to an impossible standard of perfection. However, this guide does give you a foundation to assess if that person has the skill set to help you feel emotionally, mentally, physically, and spiritually safe in a relationship. Part of that safety involves knowing that when they make a mistake, they can hold themselves accountable. They are not opposed to personal growth when needed. They also see *you* as worthy of receiving that protection and accountability.

Sometimes love addicts connect with people who are fully capable. But they treat others with more respect and care than they do the love addict. Though they have the skillset, they are showing they are available to others, just not to the love addict. Thus, it's not for the love addict to confront someone with this information, to either choose the love addict or change for them. They must take what the unavailable person is presenting and shift to relationships that do prioritize their emotional care and support.

You are seeking a healthy human who is committed to being healthy and attracting the level of health they want in others as well.

The Impact of Cultural Differences and Beliefs

Sometimes cultural differences, differing family traditions, and community practices vary between groups. Even people from the same background who grew up in the same neighborhood will have different household norms. What would be considered commonplace knowledge, etiquette, and relationship expectations for one person will vary, drastically, for the next.

This does not mean making a relationship work is impossible. It means that the people within it must make the conscious decision to intentionally learn about them. They must be curious about the other person, their whys, and what they need. As they get to know each other, if they still feel that each person fits into the mold of an available friend or partner, then moving forward is appropriate.

If the cultural or community traditions of one person directly conflict with the emotional needs and safety of the other, then a mutual decision around compatibility can be made, with love and respect for each other's differences.

There may be those with whom you have undeniable chemistry, but in the long term you are not compatible as friends or partners—and that is okay. It has no bearing on the value of the person if you find you are incompatible.

When They're Unavailable and It's Problematic

Do you show them this list of how they are not showing up for you?

It can be very tempting to show someone this list of qualities to change and sway them, especially if you are very desperate for the relationship to work out. You want them to be on the track of self-development. Or perhaps you are proactively trying to head off the impact of the red flags and signs of unavailability you see coming.

To prevent potentially predatory people from using this book as a blueprint for how and where to manipulate you with empty promises of change or even weaponizing the lists against you (back to blame-shifting), I suggest you keep this book private. Use this guide as your own means of assessment for relationships. Feel free to communicate what you need with this new language and then see what happens. See if they are able to show up in the ways you need and make a decision from there.

You cannot will a person into self-development. You also cannot threaten them, coerce them, or bribe them by using your relationship as a motivator. Self-development work *must* be entered into by a person willingly, and this process is an individual one. Sure, they may see a relationship with you as a motivator, but they will not persist if this is not a personal desire.

No one has ever entered into a mandated program for self-improvement without resentment. However, those who are ready for personal growth enter the most challenging healing journeys with hope and optimism.

Just because you see something as a problem does not mean that they do. Exposing this to them without invitation may make them feel judged, blamed, and defensive, potentially forcing them to dig more into their unavailable characteristics as a form of self-preservation and to defend themselves from you trying to control them

So, when do you share these things with someone? Are there ever any appropriate circumstances?

Yes, there are. We will talk about them in the chapter on "Communication."

When You're Tempted to Rehabilitate Them

It may be tempting—especially if those you are assessing, are those you deeply love, or would like to keep around—to attempt to use this guide as a rehabilitation plan for them.

Rather than take the information as a clear indicator of what they are emotionally and mentally capable of, you take it as a blueprint to help them become their most optimized self.

You may try to make suggestions or drop hints about what you learned are flaws. You may try to help them heal by forwarding articles and texting them the contact information of local therapists. When that doesn't work, you may use this information to threaten them that unless their behavior changes, they're gone. But this is more about controlling them than you being fed up and about to leave.

None of those plans of action are correct, as you are mistakenly trying to control the actions and behaviors of another person—which, realistically, you are unable to do—and take away their free will.

Each person is free to act and show up in the way that is their most authentic self. This does not mean their behavior is okay, but it does mean *they* get the right to choose what feels best for them and show up accordingly.

You have to decide if their best, fits your needs and standards. Nothing else.

Even if someone consistently complains about the problems they have, if they are not actively looking for solutions, they are choosing to stay where they are. Learned helplessness is a real condition that many lean into because it helps them feel control in uncontrollable circumstances.

It can be hard to believe that someone you love would be actively *choosing* to stay stuck, but here's the thing: change is hard. Sometimes staying exactly where they are is how they feel the most empowered—because they know what to expect and they know how to handle the ups and downs.

Self-development is a deeply personal process, and no one, even with good intentions, can force someone to change. Again, even if you did successfully manage to get the other person to change, the adjustments would either be short-lived or met with resentment and bitterness, as these changes were not native and authentic to the person being pressured.

They must be the one who assesses their life, decide if what they are doing is working, and if not, choose the path of recovery that feels best for them.

Chapter 15:
Communicating Your New Needs

With the new information you have about your relationships, there may be multiple conversations you feel you need to have.

You may feel called to have boundary conversations and share new revelations and updates to your previous needs. You may want to affirm and thank others for being so available to you and make attempts to move closer to them. You may want to apologize for the ways you have been unavailable and make amends. You may try to work through hurt when an available person makes a mistake, but you want to maintain the relationship.

No matter the reason, healthy communication is always key.

In this chapter, we will review how to communicate your needs for each of these scenarios. We will also focus on how to ensure you show up as your best self, and make space for others to do the same.

Communicating Your Needs to an Available Person

In reading this guide, you may find needs that you have which you not expressed to the healthy and available others in your life.

Perhaps you weren't aware these behaviors were things that you could ask for. It is also possible that you were aware that these were needs, but hesitated to ask, because you thought that you were asking for too much. Or maybe you downplayed your needs for so long that you trained your friends and loved ones to both, not consider them nor attend to your needs.

No matter the scenario, you are now ready to communicate that you want the attention and love you previously overlooked.

Sharing what you need is very important in order for the people who love you to know what your preferences are. Although healthy people are open, they are not mind readers. They may have different relationship norms than you, or they may naturally attend to some of your needs better than others. Thus, their oversight is not intentional, it's just not on their radar.

It is important to give your loved ones an opportunity to show up for you rather than internalizing feelings of rejection and abandonment, or believe they do not find your needs important. Communication is the best tool we have to grow and maintain the relationships that are most important to us.

So, how do you share this need with your loved one? Let's break this down into three simple steps:

1. Verify that this person is available, in character and action, towards you
2. Determine what it is that you need
3. Share your thoughts about your new news

Now let's dig deeper into these three steps.

Step 1: Verify that this person is available, in character and action, towards you

Before you share your new needs, you must make sure that this is a person that meets the qualifications of an Available Person. This is not to say you would not share your needs with someone who is unavailable. However, because this person is emotionally safe and open, your expectations and delivery may differ from how it may be with one who is unavailable. We will discuss the differences for those who are unavailable later in the guide.

The available people in your life have shown that they care about your emotional, physical, and mental safety. They are open to learning about you, your concerns, and what would make you feel the safest. These are the best relationships in which to make your needs known—or practice doing so for the first time—because you can trust you will not be met with a punitive or critical response that shames you for having these basic needs in the first place.

Step 2: Determine what it is that you need

From the list of available qualities, what is it that you want more of? Perhaps you would like to spend more time together? Perhaps you would like to have more physical affection? Or maybe you'd like them to keep you updated on important life events or share a bit more about what is going on with them?

Determine the exact action you want them to take to address the need, and then communicate your request clearly. A general request like, "I'd like to spend more time together," is a great start. However, what does that look like exactly? Does that mean that you would like your phone calls to go longer when you check in with them? Does that mean you'd like to have an extra date night a month? Does it mean having a monthly fun game night to build on family time together?

Reflect on your needs and why they're important to you. Sharing your feelings can help your partner understand you better and deepen your connection. If you come from a background where your needs were neglected, or you were highly criticized when younger, and adopted a more critical slant on life. If you are used to focusing on the things you don't have versus the things you do, coming up with a positive ask may be hard. You have not been trained to look at what you *do* want and what is *going right*. Your history has attuned you to seeing what is lacking in a relationship and what is going wrong.

Because of this, sharing what you *don't want* may come to your mind easier than examples of the things that you do.

Though it may be helpful to share the behaviors from the past that were hurtful, it is more productive to tell others what you need versus what you don't need. This helps give them clarity on what you are asking for and your clarity on markers to see if this person is meeting your needs in the future.

Step 3: Share your thoughts about your new needs

Now it is time to share! Preferably in person, face to face, or over the phone. Because you are expressing something that is 1) very important to you, 2) potentially brand new information, and 3) something that needs to be confirmed to be understood. I strongly suggest that you plan to share these needs with this person either in person, over the phone, or via video chat, so that you can both see each other's facial expressions and nonverbal body language.

Sharing these needs over text-only methods (i.e. e-mail, Direct Message chats, texts, social media apps, etc.) leaves way too much space for misinterpretation, and large gaps between messages. They may be perceived as rejection or hurtful to one or both sides, and a lack of understanding of the other person's emotional response to what is being asked. This method heightens the chance of someone feeling wounded, shut down, confused, attacked, or let down due to the lack of connection. That commonly happens when nonverbal body language, vocal tone, and facial expressions are unavailable.

Once you're ready to share, you do not need to create a heavy buildup leading to the conversation or tell them, "We need to talk." That phrase typically invites a lot of dread and personal defense on the part of the hearer, and you would like this conversation to remain amicable and open.

When you are in each other's presence, you can share that you have something you want to share and then express the need.

Here are some examples:

- "I know I've told you in the past that I hate phone call check-ins, but I think I would really like it if we could have them more regularly. Maybe once every few weeks, if that works for you?"

- "I know that in the past I've said I hate it when people compliment me. To be honest, it actually feels really good when I do something well and my friends celebrate me. Can you compliment me on the things that I'm proud of when I share them? You don't have to limit them anymore."

- "I didn't know how much quality time meant to me because I've spent so much of my life alone, doing things on my own. Can we have a designated friend date at least once a month? It doesn't have to be anything big. I would just love to see you in person rather than over text and social media only."

Managing Their Responses

Once you relate what you need from them, your loved one will share whether or not they are able to follow through with that ask. Some may say emphatically, "Yes!" Some may have more questions to make sure they understand, and some may validate your needs, but share that they may not be able to do it. Alternatively, they may share they are open to trying, but that what you are asking does not come naturally to them. Others may say because it does not come naturally, they are unable to meet your needs in this area.

For example, say you express the need for verbal validation. You may have a loved one who fully affirms you with ample quality time and acts of service and support. However, words are not their strong suit. Verbal expression may not be easy for them because they may be a black-and-white, matter-of-fact type of person. It is possible that they never had models of verbal kindness and compliments growing up.

This person may respond that they understand why this need is important to you, but share that it may be hard for them to do so because it's not a naturally occurring personality trait.

As shared in other places in this book, it is up to you to determine if this is a deal-breaker for the relationship or if you need to adjust your expectations and find other sources to get this need for verbal validation met.

Similarly, if you are asking for more quality time and touch points with a person but they are time-restricted due to:
- being a busy professional who travels often
- just having a child
- caretaking very sick adult parents
- any other issue that eliminates their availability

They may say that they would really love to show up for you in that way, but they cannot. You see, this is not about willful neglect, but that they simply do not have the capacity for that.

Again, you will need to assess if this is a deal-breaker or if this person meets the other markers of availability. If you feel comfortable, either adjust your expectations of them or adjust where they fit in your inner circle.

When They Can't Meet Your Needs
(But You Want to Keep the Relationship)

As expressed in this guide, when you find a close relationship meets your needs in other areas, but cannot fulfill you in a specific way, it is up to you to decide if this is a deal-breaker or not.

For some relationships, you may continue the relationship and find gratitude and appreciation for the other ways they show up. Over time, you feel that this change of perspective helps you feel satisfied to continue your relationship with them.

Others try this approach but find their sense of unfulfillment grows, eventually realizing they need something different.

Neither option is the "right" decision, as you must walk this path to learn what works best for you. However, if you choose to stay in a relationship where one of your needs cannot be met due to their lack of capacity, skill set, or willingness, you *must* make sure you are still seeking out other relationships that do supply you with that need.

It is healthy to have multiple relationships in your life that play different roles. Some may overlap in how they care for you, but no one person should be your own resource.

Also, your ultimate source of affirmation, love, and care must be yourself. Do not go without being supported or fulfilled in one area because a primary relationship cannot meet the need. This is damaging to your self-esteem and sense of self-worth.

Stay connected to yourself by seeking out relationships that show up for you fully and help you feel seen, valued, and loved.

Communicating Your Needs to an Unavailable Person

In reading this book, perhaps you have found a friend, family member, or partner to be unavailable to you. However, this is not a relationship you would like to cut ties with. You would like to use this new awareness to attempt to communicate your needs to them.

You may want to give them an opportunity to rise to the occasion and change how they show up in the relationship. Or perhaps you know they are most likely not willing to change, but you want to share your needs as a personal act of self-confidence and show up for yourself.

No matter the intention, the one thing clear is that if this person meets more qualities of an unavailable person than not, they will not be emotionally, mentally, and spiritually safe in every area of your life. You may have hope they can be this person eventually, but they are far from close.

If that is the case, let's look at how to share your needs with an unavailable person in a way that helps you preserve your integrity while protecting yourself emotionally, as much as possible.

As in the previous section, your first two steps are:

1. Determine if this person is available or unavailable
2. Determine what it is that you want

For unavailable people, the next steps differ. They are:
3. Determine how you hope this person responds to your request
4. Determine if this is a realistic expectation
5. Proactively plan for aftercare plans and support for after you have this conversation with them
6. Have the conversation with the unavailable person about your needs

We have already discussed the first two steps in detail earlier so, we will jump into discussing the next steps for communicating your needs to the unavailable.

Step 3: Determine how you hope this person responds to your request

Be honest with yourself about the type of response you want from the person who is unavailable. It may be easy to say you want to communicate your needs "just for yourself." But if you have had a relationship that has been codependent, trauma-bonded, or defined by too much emotional investment and history on your part, it is likely you have some unspoken wishes as well.

Some of those hopes may include:
- They feel guilty for what they have done
- They show some sign of sadness, regret, or contrition in their facial expressions
- They beg you to stay
- They make promises to change
- They make promises to go to therapy
- They say how they made a huge mistake and you're so important to them
- They say that the other person doesn't compare to you
- They state how they can't live without you
- They state how they will miss you
- They let you share your entire set of thoughts without interrupting you
- They let you share your entire set of thoughts without insulting you
- They say how they are happy that you shared this with them
- They say they appreciate you helping them grow/be a better person
- They apologize

Are you secretly hoping that this conversation with them produces some result other than them hearing your point of view?

Would your feelings change depending on their response? Think about the difference between them being defensive or dismissive versus welcoming and understanding.

Answer this question honestly for yourself, so you can be clear on what your hopes and expectations are. This will help you prepare yourself better for this conversation and maintain your personal integrity and emotional safety.

Step 4: Determine if this is a realistic expectation

After determining what your expectations are, it is important to get clarity on if these expectations are realistic. Included in these expectations are:

- "Do I expect this person to even give me the floor, time, or opportunity to talk to them uninterrupted?"
- If given space and time to talk, is this person someone who is willing or has the capability to hear you?

If the unavailable person has a history of the following, they will not be an emotionally safe place for you to share these needs:

- They consistently talk over you
- They make your hurt feelings about them
- They project their problems on to other people
- It is never their fault
- They are verbally abusive
- They are emotionally abusive
- They are non-responsive to you and answer with minimal words
- They are non-responsive to you and answer with silence
- They are volatile and have anger issues
- They have mentally checked out of the relationship
- They prioritize someone else's feelings over yours

- They have used you as a scapegoat and/or excluded you
- They actively use a substance that impacts their ability to receive and process information
- They are battling a mental illness without outside intervention, which impacts their ability to receive and process information
- They do not like you as a person
- They think they are better than you
- They think your emotions are exaggerated and you're too sensitive
- They have sought to have control over and dominate you in the past in any way (i.e. mentally, emotionally, physically, financially, spiritually, sexually, etc.)

There are countless ways that an unavailable person may have shown signs to you that they are not emotionally safe for you. It is important that you pay attention to these signs. Be aware; just because you are ready to show up in your strength, it does not mean they will bend to your will and be receptive and open to you.

This does not necessarily mean that you should not use your voice and share your needs. Your voice and your ability to advocate for yourself are the most important traits for you to develop.

This step simply asks for you to examine that as you consider stepping into this conversation with this person, you are clear on the reality of who you are talking to and what you will be facing.

You may be adding to the pain, you may have had in the past when this person has been inattentive or hurtful to your needs. If you were to share your feelings vulnerably with an expectation of them to be thoughtful, considerate, apologetic, fair, or repentant and they were not, the amount of hurt you would receive would be twice as much.

If you find that this person has any of the previously mentioned behaviors or is indifferent, dismissive, or belittling, and you decide to still talk with them, ensure you are doing so *only* to utilize the power of your voice. Ensure that the only validation you are seeking is your own. You must either be unbothered by the other's response or have prepared resources to support you in the case of their response being hurtful (See Step 5).

Without all these expectations, you are less likely to end up in a back-and-forth exchange, fight, or heartbreak, as you were not expecting any response from them in either direction.

If you find that validation is something you do crave from this interaction, see Figure 15.1, "A Note About Wanting Validation."

A Note About Wanting Validation

With those who have previously shown that they are unavailable and do not care to attend to your needs, be mindful of attempting to communicate your unmet needs to be validated, heard, or having your experience <u>finally</u> be justified.

You don't need for them to do that. Your experience is already important, and it is your own. You are already worthy. *Your feelings matter.*

Communication at this point must be based on you showing up for yourself and correcting your own harmful or inappropriate behaviors.

When love addicts come from a people-pleasing and codependent background, you are taught to negotiate with those who undervalue you. You learn that it is somehow your responsibility to coerce the other person into seeing enough value in you to respect you and hear you out.

You already have inherent value. If they do not see it, that is a THEM problem, not a YOU problem. Also, if the y are treating you in a way that marks off multiple items from the Unavailable list, their bad behavior is due to where they are on their personal journey, and not that you deserve this treatment.

Figure 15.1

Step 5: Proactively plan for aftercare plans and support after you have this conversation with them.

Make plans to have an available person check in with right before you share these needs with this person, and also right after.

This person should be validating, supportive, and understanding of your needs. They should be someone who has clear boundaries and advocates for you to show up for yourself.

When talking with an unavailable person, it may be a bit nerve-racking, especially if this is your first time advocating for yourself or using your voice. You may be nervous about their response or if you will be able to communicate what you need clearly. Perhaps you are fearful of rejection or other forms of retaliation. Or perhaps previous emotional abuse and neglect have caused you to doubt that your points of view are valid. You may be susceptible to either the unavailable person's dismissive responses or your own internal voices that make you doubt yourself and think that you're asking for too much.

For these reasons, bookmarking your conversation with external support is imperative for your own emotional care. Even if you feel you do not need the emotional support, having someone to debrief with will give you an external perspective. It will be invaluable to help you remain grounded and connected to your own feelings and point of view.

For example, if you know you're going to have an important conversation with a romantic partner on Tuesday afternoon, you can pre-plan with a supportive girlfriend. Let her know when you're about to go talk to your partner and let her know that you will call her afterwards and update her about how it goes. She should understand that you need her to help you process your conversation.

If you have a therapist you trust, you can proactively process an important conversation you want to have with a friend who has been a bit triggering. You can then either follow up with your therapist after the conversation or enlist the help of another friend to debrief afterwards.

Step 6: Have a conversation with the unavailable person about your needs.

For an unavailable person, because they have a history of not being a safe space, nor do they proactively attend to your needs, it is important to be prepared. With that said, I encourage you to share your boundaries for the conversation before you share these needs.

Boundaries are not commands of what the other person should do or say. Boundaries are when you share what you need to feel safe and what you will do if you feel those boundaries are not being respected. Boundaries are all about exhibiting limits on the only person you have control over—yourself.

Thus, if you do not feel safe or heard, in any part of the conversation, it is up to you to follow through with the steps needed to help you feel safe.

An example of how to open a conversation about boundaries may sound like: "I have something I need to share with you, and I need to be able to do so without you interrupting me or insulting what I have to say. If that happens, I will end the conversation and leave."

Note that this share with the unavailable person is to inform, not to get their approval or permission on the boundary that is being set. Thus, there is no need to go back and forth with them before starting. If they are not open to respecting the boundary, then you are able to opt out at any time. At any time, you may maintain your emotional safety and integrity by choosing to end the conversation or exit.

The Possible Responses

Open to Hear You–Implements Changes

When you share your needs with the unavailable person, some may be open to hear your desires. They may express their unawareness of not meeting your need, make their apologies and be open to taking the next steps to show up for you in the way you need.

Should their response be genuine, you will find that this change is long term. It is not dependent on their own personal hang-ups and issues. They will do the work, be self-accountable for creating this change, and seek out their own resources and support to make changes in this area.

Even if you choose to revisit this conversation in the future, you are not the one who is in charge of reminding them of their commitment. Nor do you need to initiate and schedule when they will follow up with you.

You see that this pivot is internally motivated by wanting to provide this safe space for you, and it does not fade over time.

Open to Hear You–Starts off Feigning Change–But Returns to Normal

For this response, the person is open and receptive to what you have to say. They may express they were unaware and/or take ownership for the gaps in their awareness. They will also make a commitment to change.

To start, you will notice this person making attempts to change. Whether their promise is to be more expressive, more available time-wise, more responsive, or thoughtful, you see real actions behind the words.

However, over time, their actions begin to falter. You, seeing the original change, may be tempted to remind them of their commitment to you and how these oversights make you feel.

Then the person may express understanding and temporarily change or give an excuse that they are working on it and doing their best.

This cycle continues until you are back at the beginning, with your need being unmet and the person totally back in their unavailable state. They may still give verbal promises and assurances about the change, but there are no actions. If pressed, they may become resistant and defensive of your lack of acknowledgement of the previous changes.

If this cycle happens for you, be mindful that this person is not indebted to unconditional gratitude for initially treating you with the love and respect you asked for. All needs listed in this book are basic minimum standards for all relationships.

If this person is unable to meet the need you requested, consistently, it is up to you to decide where you will place this person in your life, knowing they are not available in this area.

Resistant to Hear You/Defensive

If they meet the qualifiers of the Unavailable list of this book, this person may not be receptive to your boundaries nor your requests for your new needs. Even if they initially agree, the unavailable person may attempt to get you to negotiate them once you start sharing or afterwards by:

- poking holes to show how you are being unreasonable
- lamenting about how you're hurting *them* and being unfair to *their* experience
- criticizing you and calling you selfish
- pushing familiar buttons to get you to adjust your boundaries so that they can continue to treat you in the way they are accustomed to

If this is their response, be mindful of any urge to explain your position and get them to see your point of view. You do not need their approval that your feelings are valid. They are entitled to their standards, and you are entitled to yours. If they do not align, that simply means your relationship, as it currently stands, is not a match.

Also, as a person who has been unavailable to you, 9.99999 times out of 10 they will not see your point of view. And if they do, they will not affirm it because then it means they will have to change.

As a reminder, the only person you can control is yourself. You are the only one who is charged with ensuring you are in a safe, loving relationship. You do that by adjusting your environment when you find the relationships you are in do not align with that basic right of safety, love, and protection.

If this person is either unable to or unwilling to care for you in the way that you need, you can make space for those who will.

Self-Assessment Questions

- Are there any people in your life that you would like to share your new needs with? Would you consider them available towards you or unavailable?
- What are the standards and boundaries needed to ensure a conversation about sharing your needs is safe to participate in?
- What do you feel may be the easiest part about having these conversations? What would be the hardest parts?

Chapter 16:
How to Apologize and Make Amends

So, upon reflection, you realize that *you* may have been the one whose actions were hurtful to a relationship. While you could try to ignore it and move on, you understand that acknowledging the harm would go a long way to repairing any lost trust.

Having these hard conversations can feel unfamiliar and awkward. But learning how to face your mistakes, hold your value, and offer the space for others to have their own experience is deeply healing.

In healthy relationships, it is not required that both people are perfect. However, what is required is having an open line of communication for both sides to be vulnerable when needed. There must be space for both persons to show up and make amends when needed for the relationship to grow and change.

So, let's talk about how you can make amends to the important people in your life.

The three general steps of making amends are:

1. Acknowledge and take ownership of your actions (and their impact on the other person)
2. Apologize and offer empathy by validating their right to be hurt
3. Make real changes on your own or enlist the help of another to help ensure that the behaviors are not repeated

Let's break these down a bit.

Step 1: Acknowledge and take ownership of what happened

Write out the actions or behaviors that you did in the relationship for which you would like to apologize.

As you write this list, you may remember the situation's details and feelings that led to this behavior. This is great information for your context, but do not plan to lead with this when making amends to your person. Should you do so, these details may become an excuse to rationalize and minimize what happened.

Repeat this process with any other persons you would like to acknowledge your previous behaviors to so that you can move on.

If you notice that there is a recurring pattern of behaviors with similar triggers across relationships, it may be helpful to explore these behaviors in therapy to fully break these habits and heal the roots that cause them. This will prohibit them from resurfacing in your current and future relationships.

Step 2: Apologize for the impact

Actively saying the words "I am sorry for" or "I apologize for" and then following with the action that you did is significant. For example:

> *"I am sorry that I have not been available for our phone call check-ins."*

> *"I apologize for dominating our conversations and not asking about how you're doing."*

Statements like, "I'm sorry if you felt bad for what I did," are *not* an apology. They insinuate that the blame is on the person for being hurt and absolves you from admitting that what you did was hurtful.

An alternative example for this apology is this simple script:

> *I have been thinking and realize that in the past I have [insert unavailable actions].*

> *Though my intention was not to hurt you, I understand that my actions may have made you feel [insert the emotions you imagine they may have felt], in the past.*

> *I want to say I'm sorry for these things and I would like to work towards being more available to your needs in the future.*

After you apologize, if it feels appropriate, you may share the context of what was going on with you that led to this issue. (e.g. "This is the first healthy relationship I've had with someone who cared about what I have felt, so it is new for me to share.") But make sure to leave space for the other person to respond and either accept or decline your apology.

It is okay for the person to say they need time to think about what you shared. Ideally, your primary intention must be to make this person feel seen, safe, and valued. You may want reconciliation, but if the person is not ready to talk about pursuing the next steps right now, forcing it may make the situation escalate. And it will diffuse the goodwill you just imparted.

Allow this person the space to decide if you need to come back together. If they are open to discussing more, you can progress to Step 3.

Step 3: Share your plan of action for making amends

In this step, you will share what you will do going forward to attempt to correct this action. This share can be as short as "I will be mindful of this in the future." Or it can be as detailed as a planned set of next steps you will take to remedy it. It is up to you. However, the fact that this person now knows that you understand the impact of what has happened and have taken their needs into consideration is huge.

Keep in mind, however, that sometimes we think we know what the other person needs, and this may end up being the opposite of what they really desire. So, in this conversation, it is wiser to ask directly what they need from you in this area. They may affirm that they just need to feel heard, or they may have a specific ask of you. Listen, and ensure it is something you can commit to. In this way, you may prevent any future conflicts.

It is also possible that the person on the receiving end may not consider this a big deal and has already forgiven you. They may have a high level of personal confidence and are not fazed by others' human mistakes.

These grounded souls are some of the *best* friends and partners, especially for those who are codependent, as they provide a good model of self-assuredness.

When They Have Feedback for You, in Return

Sometimes, the person's response will be feedback that is critical. This feedback may not always be attacking, but simply honest. This feedback may be strong because they want you to have honest information and help you grow, to know how to reconcile the relationship. If this is the case, the conversation will be hard to hear, but constructive.

Use your discernment to decide what to take in and what to leave. If the feedback is constructive, use it to move forward with your person, to build a healthier communication and connection style between you. If critical and abusive, assess whether this relationship would be a safe space to continue investing in.

Self-Assessment Questions

- Are there any people with whom you'd like to make amends for ways you were unavailable or may have harmed your relationship with them?
- If you were on the receiving end of some of your actions, what do you think you would need from the other person?
- What can you do to prepare yourself to be open to any feedback from the person(s) you're making amends with?

Chapter 17:
Where to Find Available People

After clearing out relationships that are unavailable, you will have space for new relationships—those who are healthy and available for you. However, many love addicts, especially early on in their healing journey, either 1) do not have many available people to practice building relationships with, or 2) do not know where to find them.

If this is the case for you, here's a step-by-step process to find those who are available.

Step 1: Become available yourself

If you have been surrounded by mostly unavailable people, you may have some hidden habits that have made you more susceptible to unavailable relationships. To become available, targeting the root source of these hidden habits will help you become more available to those who are healthy and open to fulfilling partnerships and friendships.

Here are four common hidden habits that make it easier for you to connect to and prioritize relationships with unavailable people:

Four Hidden Attractors to Unavailable Relationships

1. You are not attuned to healthy love and may continue to subconsciously find unavailable people who cannot give you what you need because that is what you're most familiar with.

2. The pain and betrayal from past unavailable relationships make it difficult to be open and trust future healthy relationships.

3. Your self-worth may be very low and is partly why you did not previously catch the undervaluing treatment by unavailable people as you did not think you deserved more.

4. You subconsciously benefited from unavailable relationships because they never required you to be truly vulnerable because all attention was on the other person and the relationship.

To maintain these relationships on a long-term basis, you learned the art of self-neglect and abandoning yourself, even if it was subconscious. To correct this, you must gain the skill set to learn how to identify your needs, feel as if they are worthy, stand in them, and give them wholeheartedly to yourself first.

Things that shouldn't have been normalized for you, so until you work on them, it may be very difficult to be attracted to available people, due to previous hurt and trauma.

Healthy love and attention may seem foreign, excessive, or too good to be true. You may confuse the actions of an interested and available partner with the love-bombing tactics of a narcissist. Your unresolved abandonment wounds may cause you to create or look for reasons to leave and end a relationship before they leave you first. Low self-worth may also make you think you are unworthy of such good behavior, which pushes away the very acts you have wanted to receive.

For you to be a match for the relationships you want, you must become available yourself by working on the traumas that underline this. Here are the target healing actions for each of those common hidden habits:

Target Healing Actions to Become Available

1) You are not attuned to healthy love and may continue to subconsciously find unavailable people who cannot give you what you need because that is what you're most familiar with.

Target healing action: Start to prioritize your emotional and physical needs and give them to yourself first before giving to others

2) The pain and betrayal from past unavailable relationships makes it difficult to be open and trust future healthy relationships

Target healing action: Heal from the trauma of betrayal from past relationships. Deconstruct old narratives that you cannot trust people or that love hurts and create new stories that healthy love is available to you

3) Your self-worth may be very low and is partly the reason why you did not previously catch the undervaluing treatment by unavailable people as you did not think you deserved more

Target healing action: Heal symptoms of childhood emotional neglect or related trauma where your needs were not prioritized. Start to build a healthy self-concept that you are worthy of being adored and valued.

4) You subconsciously benefited from unavailable relationships because they never required you to be truly vulnerable. All attention was on the other person in the relationship

Target healing action: Heal the tendency to hide from being attended to in primary relationships and learn to ask for what you need consistently and often

This process seems and looks tedious. In over fifteen years as a licensed therapist and eight years of psychoeducational coaching, I have found that if you give women the right tools, they will take it from there.

I help my clients work on the four hidden attractors of unavailable relationships and the root causes in my Love Addiction Recovery School Coaching Program. In this program, I have helped hundreds of women. I show them how to heal from love addiction, love avoidance, love deprivation, and the trauma it causes to make way for healthy love in their lives.

I am both a mental health professional *and* a woman who had to go through her own healing and recovery process. I have learned the importance of integrating trauma work with learning new skills and changing one's behavior.

Through this program, women unlearn the roots of these intimacy disorders that have attracted them to unhealthy relationships. They conquer the limiting beliefs that keep them stuck and learn how to grow available relationships with others while not abandoning themselves.

Should you want more help in working through these subconscious habits to be free, you can learn more and enroll at TheRecoverySchool.com

Step 2: Start to build your life based on things you want to do

Building a relationship with yourself where you are actively pursuing things that make you laugh, make you light up, and give you pleasure, brings its own level of joy and contentment.

This level of joy opens you up to becoming happier and more fulfilled. Happier and fulfilled people are not only magnetic to others, but they are more grounded and available for new connections when ready.

Once you know what lights you up, building a routine around these hobbies and interests will help you cultivate a community and relationships centered on what already gives you joy in your life.

But I'm an introvert!

Whether your interests are more introverted than extroverted, this opportunity is available to you. Do you love reading books about historical romance? There are book clubs in real life or online, available for you. Love watching sports? Find a local sports bar that matches your vibe and go there consistently for the big game. Have you always wanted to knit but never had time? Start knitting and connect with a knitting club on social media that sometimes meets up at a coffee shop to sit and knit—talking optional.

The Importance of Finding and Grounding Yourself

You must first find yourself to truly find your people. Otherwise, you risk connecting with people with whom you share no meaningful bond or common foundation. If you tend to become overly accommodating in order to connect with others, you may end up adopting the personalities and interests of those around you rather than fully embracing your true self.

You need to be your whole self in order to correctly assess who you are a good match with. After you determine availability, this is where the fun stuff like a sense of humor, chemistry, joint interests, and vibes come into play.

Finding Your Tribe Through Habit and Consistency

To find community relationships, your best tool will be consistency. If you are going out to sports bars to support your team, but every week it's a new location, you will be starting from scratch each time. You will also have a harder time assessing someone's personality from one interaction. And if you're already an introvert, putting pressure on yourself to initiate conversations with new people every other week is setting yourself up for failure.

Find your interests and become a regular there. As you create your life, you *will* find your tribe.

Step 3: Initiate the closeness and be a mirror of what you would like to receive

Once connected, be the kind of friend, partner, or family member you would like to be on the receiving end of.

If you want to have phone calls and check-ins, initiate these connections with them yourself. If you want compliments and verbal affirmations, are you giving them to your friends as well, or just waiting to receive them? When you receive them, do you tell your people how much you like it and how loved it makes you feel? If you want to be celebrated when positive things happen, are you remembering and celebrating your friends as well?

We must put out the energy we'd like to receive.

How do you use this guide for new people in your life?

For new acquaintances, there's no need to rush to learn everything about them right away. Time will show you someone's character and values.

Research shows that it takes 80 hours of contact for us to build a deep friendship. This is why it seems like it is easier to make friends at work or when we are in school—we are around these people for extended periods of time. With that said, do not get discouraged if you meet someone you could be great friends with, but it's taking time to grow and nurture the friendship. In this busy world, it *should* take some time. Just worry about your side of the street, stay intentional with your part by initiating connections, and see what grows.

You will learn about this person as you spend time together; the stories they tell will reveal their values, how they interact in other relationships, and their temperament styles

It may be tempting to gather as much information as you can about someone, to see if they pass the test of availability right away. However, the nature of a person's character is revealed through time and consistent contact. Only then will you learn if their first impression actually reflects how they show up in relationships or was merely enough to get you hooked.

Sometimes, someone who starts off very generous may eventually start to punish you or feel resentful of their past actions, using these things as reasons to criticize you.

On the other hand, a friend who starts off reserved may eventually be able to open up to you as you spend more time together. It is not that they are unavailable, but introverted and may simply need more time to let you in or share their inner thoughts. What they need is the time to grow and slowly build trust.

Love Addicts and Going Slow Getting to Know Someone

If you struggle with love addiction, it may be hard for you to slow down the "get to know you" process due to the urgency to 1) ensure someone is "safe" and 2) feel fully connected.

If you struggle with love avoidance, this may be hard for you. It may be tempting to keep others who show signs of availability at arm's length until they pass the 40-point checklist test to see if they are worth letting in.

Avoid urges to go super-slow or super-fast. Just allow yourself to be present in the moment. Enjoy learning more about them little by little, and showing them what feels open and safe about yourself. Others will always reveal their character over time, and you will be able to make decisions from there.

Pay Attention to How They Treat Others

Please note that for all relationships, it is important for you to pay attention to how this person treats others as an indicator of how they will treat you. If they are dishonest towards others and often tell little lies of omission, the same will happen for you. If they talk negatively about those in their inner circle to you, you will also be discussed negatively one day when they are not around.

Character is consistent. When someone shows you and tells you who they are, believe them, and do not think yourself to be the exception.

Self-Assessment Questions

- Do you prefer to instantly connect with others or get to know them slowly over time?
- Can you relate to any of the four hidden attractors to unavailable relationships? If so, which ones?
- Which of the targeted actions for healing would you like to prioritize first?
- Do you know what lights you up and makes you happy? If wanting to make more relationships based on mutual interests, do you have any hobbies or have interests where you could involve others or seek interest groups?

Shena Lashey, M.MFT

Chapter 18:
Conclusion–You Got This

I am so proud of you for doing the work to make a real change and transform your relationships. It is absolutely worth the effort, and I know you will receive everything that you are worth and more.

This guide has helped you learn the difference between unavailable and available characteristics. Now you can make informed decisions on which relationships to keep close and which to move away from.

Use the information on the qualities of availability to assess both yourself and your primary relationships, regularly. Make sure you are showing up for each other in full. In this guide, you have learned how to use these qualities for your own personal growth. You have also learned to use them as a tool to express to your loved ones what you need in your connections to feel safe, loved, and seen.

You learned the qualities of unavailable people, what makes these actions so harmful, and how to express your needs to others. For those who would like to communicate your newly found needs, we broke down how to approach these conversations with both available and unavailable people and how the method may vary along with our expectations. We also studied how to make amends if we find we are the harming partner. And how we can continue to grow the relationships that mean the most to us.

Finally, we discovered where to go to find those who are available to us. For those of us who have hidden attractors toward unavailable relationships, you now have the guidance to identify these factors and also how to repair these wounds for your future.

There is a saying by German theologian Martin Luther that goes, "You cannot stop the birds from flying above your head, but you can stop them from making a nest in your hair." It is up to you to pay attention to the warning signs for those who are unavailable. Take heed rather than dismissing them and allowing them to take root in your life.

Simultaneously, make space in your heart for the people who are ready and willing to love you. You deserve to have healthy love, friendships, and partnerships that last and add to the fulfillment in each of your lives.

I am forever rooting for you. You got this!

Additional Resources

How to Pick Partners Free Resources

You will find additional resources, checklists, and free downloads for this book at HowToPickPartners.com

How to Pick Partners Workbook

For a full workbook to break down the entire process of assessing your relationships, your personal availability qualities, hidden attractors of unavailable relationships, finding your joy and more, check out the companion guidebook—*How to Pick Partners for Love Addicts Workbook.*

Learn more at HowToPickPartners.com

Heal from Love Addiction and Trauma

To heal the symptoms of love addiction, love avoidance, and the trauma that causes it, check out **the Love Addiction Recovery School**–the leading online Love Addiction Recovery Program for those ready to heal their self-esteem and get the relationships they want. Learn more at TheRecoverySchool.com.

About the Author

Shena Lashey is a dedicated expert in relational trauma and love addiction, serving as a Coach and Licensed Professional Counselor in Houston, TX.

With over 15 years of experience as a Licensed Therapist, as the visionary founder of Black Girls Heal, she passionately guides women of color in breaking free from patterns of unhealthy relationships and love addiction.

Shena's innovative Healed and Loved Woman Framework™ provides a clear pathway for healing childhood trauma and cultivating profound self-love.

Through her compelling podcast, Black Girls Heal, Shena engages millions of listeners around the world in crucial conversations about intimacy, attachment, and emotional wellness.

Her transformative coaching programs and events including The Love Addiction Recovery School & Healed & Loved Woman Retreat empower women with actionable strategies to reclaim their lives, positioning Shena as an inspiring force for change and healing in the lives of those she serves.

Printed in Great Britain
by Amazon

55694212R00096